PORTRAITS of Jewish-American HEROES

MALKA DRUCKER

Illustrated by

ELIZABETH ROSEN

Dutton Children's Books

Dutton Children's Books

A DIVISION OF PENGUIN YOUNG READERS GROUP

PUBLISHED BY THE PENGUIN GROUP

Penguin Group (USA) Inc., 375 Hudson Street, New York, New York 10014, U.S.A. / Penguin Group (Canada), 90 Eglinton Avenue East, Suite 700, Toronto, Ontario, Canada M4P 2Y3 (a division of Pearson Penguin Canada Inc.) / Penguin Books Ltd, 80 Strand, London WC2R 0RL, England / Penguin Ireland, 25 St Stephen's Green, Dublin 2, Ireland (a division of Penguin Books Ltd) / Penguin Group (Australia), 250 Camberwell Road, Camberwell, Victoria 3124, Australia (a division of Pearson Australia Group Pty Ltd) / Penguin Books India Pvt Ltd, 11 Community Centre, Panchsheel Park, New Delhi - 110 017, India / Penguin Group (NZ), 67 Apollo Drive, Rosedale, North Shore 0632, New Zealand (a division of Pearson New Zealand Ltd) / Penguin Books (South Africa) (Pty) Ltd, 24 Sturdee Avenue, Rosebank, Johannesburg 2196, South Africa / Penguin Books Ltd, Registered Offices: 80 Strand, London WC2R 0RL, England

Text copyright © 2008 by Malka Drucker
Illustrations copyright © 2008 by Elizabeth Rosen

Library of Congress Cataloging-in-Publication Data
Drucker, Malka.
Portraits of Jewish-American heroes / by Malka Drucker; illustrated by Elizabeth Rosen.
p. cm.
Includes bibliographical references.
ISBN: 978-0-525-47771-6
1. Jews—United States—Biography—Juvenile literature.
2. Jewish women—United States—Biography—Juvenile literature. I. Rosen, Elizabeth, date. II. Title.
E184.37.A133 2008   973'.04924—dc22   [B]   2007028481

Published in the United States by Dutton Children's Books,
a division of Penguin Young Readers Group
345 Hudson Street, New York, New York 10014
www.penguin.com/youngreaders

Designed by Heather Wood
Manufactured in China / First Edition

1 3 5 7 9 10 8 6 4 2

ART NOTE I used different media to create these portraits, to tell of each hero's life. For instance, Haym Salomon was built with pillars, wood, and tiles. Levi Strauss was painted on denim and finished with sewn details. Harry Houdini was painted on aged wood with nails to imitate a sign he might have displayed. Einstein's brilliance was created in an energetic collage. The original art varies widely in size—some are four inches, and some are four feet! I loved working on this book. I learned much, felt much, and spread my wings artistically.

FOR

Rabbi Harold M. Schulweis,
who keeps me believing in heroes.
To my first heroes, my father and mother,
William and Francine.

M.D.

FOR

Another Jewish hero, my father, Harris Rosen,
who taught me patience, generosity, strength, and how to rise
above difficult situations with dignity. And for Toni Henderson
who was my community when I had none, and who
selflessly, happily drove this to the finish line.

E.R.

ACKNOWLEDGMENTS Although only one name usually appears as the author of a book, it takes many people for its creation. Stephanie Lurie, who suggested the project to me and who edited this book into its final polish, deserves greatest gratitude. Although their suggestions of the Beastie Boys, Emma Goldman, and Bob Dylan didn't make the list, I thank my children, Ivan and Max, and their partners, Caroline and Betsy, for their help and creativity. Thanks to Sylvia Boorstein, Michael Gold, and Howard Maisel for their suggestions of heroes and criteria for heroism. Samoa Wallach was both a scholarly researcher and an intrepid detective in this project. My congregation, HaMakom, helps me to witness ordinary heroism through their lives. And always, my life-partner, Gay Block, listened to the stories of each hero and gave boundless enthusiasm and encouragement.

CONTENTS

To the Reader . . . 6

Haym Salomon . . . 9

Levi Strauss . . . 13

Emma Lazarus . . . 17

Louis Dembitz Brandeis . . . 21

Henrietta Szold . . . 25

Rachel "Ray" Frank . . . 29

Lillian Wald . . . 33

Harry Houdini
(Ehrich Weiss) . . . 37

Albert Einstein . . . 41

Golda Meir . . . 45

ABRAHAM JOSHUA HESCHEL . . . 49

HENRY BENJAMIN "HANK" GREENBERG . . . 53

LEONARD BERNSTEIN . . . 57

BELLA SAVITSKY ABZUG . . . 61

RUTH BADER GINSBURG . . . 65

GLORIA STEINEM . . . 69

MICHAEL SCHWERNER &
ANDREW GOODMAN . . . 73

STEVEN SPIELBERG . . . 77

JUDITH ARLENE RESNIK . . . 81

DANIEL PEARL . . . 85

GLOSSARY . . . 88

JEWISH-AMERICAN HISTORY TIMELINE . . . 91

BIBLIOGRAPHY . . . 94

SUGGESTED READING (FOR AGES 10 AND UP) . . . 95

To the Reader

When I was growing up, biographies were my favorite kind of book. Reading about great people who were once small and inexperienced, encouraged me not to give up when I felt defeated. They helped me to imagine the kind of person I wanted to be. Most inspiring were not their achievements but the difficulties that they had to overcome.

The twenty outstanding people you'll find in this book faced obstacles, too. Albert Einstein struggled in school. Leonard Bernstein's father didn't want him to be a musician. Judith Resnik and Steven Spielberg suffered the trauma of divorcing parents. Golda Meir, Levi Strauss, and Harry Houdini came from poor, illiterate immigrant families.

This is a book about heroes, not simply famous people. We live in an age of celebrity, and it's easy to confuse fame with greatness. Being a football star, rock singer, or even president of the United States doesn't make somebody a hero. While it doesn't always take the form of risking one's life for another human being, heroism requires the courage to speak the truth when no one wants to hear it, to stand up for the weak, and to risk ridicule by doing something new to make the world better. Heroes set an example of the best a human being can do, and they work not only for themselves but also for others.

The people profiled in this book represent different areas of achievement, including music, entertainment, science, sports, education, and business. Regardless of their gifts, most of them were passionate about social justice. Many were not particularly religious, yet their lives reflect the high value that Judaism places on making an unfair world fairer.

Supreme Court Justices Louis Brandeis and Ruth Bader Ginsburg, Congresswoman Bella Abzug, and Lillian Wald used law as a shield against injustice. Michael Schwerner and Andrew Goodman gave their lives in the fight for African-American civil rights. Albert Einstein was a peace activist in his later years. Emma Lazarus's words at the base of the Statue of Liberty immortalize the hope and promise of America for all immigrants.

The people in this book tell the story of what it means to be both a Jew and an American. For most Jewish Americans, their story begins with immigration—their own, their parents', or their grandparents'. Imagine how difficult it must have been for them to adjust to life in a new country when they had little money, were ignorant of the language and customs, and were faced with prejudice. Despite the challenges, American Jews, who make up only 2 percent of the population, have contributed mightily to our society. While some of the heroes are more connected to Judaism and the Jewish people than others, every portrait is of a person who was proud to be a Jew.

From its beginnings, America, founded on religious freedom, has been a land of opportunity for Jews socially as well as spiritually. But even freedom poses challenge. While Revolutionary War patriot Haym Sa-

lomon fought for a nation where Jews could be full citizens, he feared that Judaism in the new country would disappear as Jews left their traditions to become Americans.

He would have been pleased to know that in the more than 350 years that Jews have lived in America, they have added a vibrant chapter to Jewish history and have enriched the melting pot of cultures unique to this country. When Rabbi Abraham Joshua Heschel marched for the civil rights of African-Americans, it was a great day to be an American and a Jew.

Even in America, everyone in this book knew the sting of anti-Semitism. Most came from poor families, and women had to overcome gender prejudice, too. Still, the opportunities were greater than in any other country in which Jews had lived, and many took them to do great things. Why someone becomes a hero is a mystery that some call God. I write of these people to honor their work and with the hope that their achievements will inspire future heroes.

Haym Salomon

1740
TO
1785

When Haym Salomon, the first Polish Jew to come to America, stepped off the boat that brought him to New York in 1772, his years of wandering through Europe finally ended. At age thirty-two, he had found the place where he belonged, a place that offered the most precious gift: the opportunity to better one's life. America was a new land of adventurous pioneers in search of religious and economic freedom. In Europe, Jews were forced to pay extra taxes and live in special neighborhoods, and sometimes they were prohibited from practicing their traditions.

There were different challenges for Jews in the New World. Although there were no laws that persecuted Jews, most people were Christian. The Sabbath was Sunday, not Saturday, and there were very few synagogues. In a letter home, Haym complained to his father that there was very little *Yiddishkeit*—the word Eastern European Jews used to describe Jewishness—in the New World. Jewish children would learn more about their tradition in Europe, he wrote.

Bright and ambitious, Haym soon joined the Sons of Liberty, a group of young men fighting to free America from British rule. His store, which sold everything from blankets to flour, became a secret meeting place for the group. The British soldiers swarming the streets watched the store very carefully for suspicious activity, but Haym was able to sneak young Colonials—American freedom fighters—out of the city to escape arrest by the British.

In 1777, Haym married Rachel Franks, who came from a prominent Sephardic family. Her brother was a colonel under George Washington. Soon after their wedding, the British imprisoned Haym, falsely accusing him of helping to set a fire that destroyed much of New York. Rachel feared that her husband would be hanged like Nathan Hale, another patriot who had worked as a spy.

But Haym's early journeys saved his life. He had learned ten languages by the time he came to America, and when the British discovered his skill, they released him from prison to be an interpreter for the German soldiers they had paid to fight the Colonials. Haym couldn't believe his good luck! Every time he spoke with a German, he would ask the soldier why he wasn't fighting for the Colonials. If you joined us, Haym told them, you could fight for your own freedom in the New World.

When the British realized what he was doing, they arrested him again, three weeks after the birth of his first child, Eliezer. This time they convicted him of spying and sabotage, and sentenced him to be hanged. Haym escaped prison with the help of a young German soldier and fled to Philadelphia, leaving his business and family behind.

Soon Rachel and the baby were able to join him in the new city. There he once again became a successful businessman, who received money in the form of gold through lending and investment. The new government of the Colonies, the Continental Congress, was desperate for food and clothing for its soldiers, but there was no Treasury yet. They gave Haym paper money in exchange for gold that they used to buy supplies. The paper money was a promise for repayment in gold. Haym wasn't the only wealthy Colonist, but he more than anyone wanted to help the new government with his riches.

Whenever the government was short of money, the first cry was, "Send for Haym Salomon!" He was proud of his title of Broker for the Office of Finance. Some early settlers, however, brought the old prejudice against Jews to the new country. They accused Haym of getting rich by charging interest on the money that was borrowed from him. Of course, it was untrue. He became wealthy not for himself but so that he could help the Colonies gain freedom. By the end of the war, he had lent the government over $353,000.

Haym balanced his devotion to America with his love of Judaism. On Yom Kippur, the holiest day of the Jewish year, Haym was leading the service when a messenger sent by George Washington arrived and begged for money for hungry soldiers. Haym stopped the prayers and asked the congregation for pledges of money for the troops. When they had raised enough, he continued the service.

As Haym worked day and night for the

government to give them all the gold they needed, he grew weak. His previous imprisonments in damp, cold jail cells had destroyed his lungs. He died at forty-five, leaving his wife with four small children, the youngest born two weeks after Haym's death.

Rachel was exhausted by grief, but she wasn't concerned that her husband had left her with no money. She had his assurance that the Continental Congress had promised to repay the money he had lent to the government. Unfortunately, however, the loan was never repaid. Haym Solomon's contribution to his beloved country was ignored until 1941, when the city of Chicago erected a statue of him standing beside George Washington.

LEVI STRAUSS

FEBRUARY 26, 1829
TO
SEPTEMBER 26, 1902

If there is one piece of clothing that most people, regardless of nationality, gender, or age, have worn, it is blue jeans. For this garment, which is as American as our flag, we have Levi Strauss to thank. He was a young immigrant when he came to New York in 1847 from Buttenheim, Germany.

Levi's father died when he was a teenager. As the eldest son, Levi struggled to support his family. Working as a peddler of needles, pins, threads, and cloth, Levi strapped a fifty-pound pack on his back and another one on his chest and went door-to-door to sell his goods. On rainy days, his feet dragged through muddy streets and his back ached from the weight of a wet pack. Barely making enough money for food, Levi convinced his mother and siblings to leave Germany for America.

In New York, he continued to peddle, but in those days many Jews were peddlers, and the competition for customers was tremendous. When Levi heard that thousands of people were racing to California to become gold miners, he packed up his goods and arrived in San Francisco in 1853.

There he met miners eager to buy anything he had to sell, for higher prices than he could charge in New York. He found that he could sell his products for even more money outside San Francisco, in the little towns where the miners worked. One of the most popular items he sold was heavy canvas that the miners used for tents.

One day Levi was sitting beside the Sacramento River eating lunch when a miner asked him what he was selling. After refusing all his goods, the miner said that what he really needed were strong pants that would hold pieces of gold. Never one to turn down a potential customer, Levi measured the man's legs and told him to come back later.

In a nearby mining town, he quickly found a tailor who took the tent canvas and made the pair of pants according to Levi's instructions, with big pockets that could hold gold and tools. The miner was so pleased that he gave Levi six dollars in gold dust, and soon other miners began to ask for "those pants of Levi's." Within a year, Levi had opened a store in San Francisco

with his brother-in-law called Levi Strauss and Company.

Miners weren't the only ones who wore Levi's pants. Cowboys liked the way the garment felt when they rode horses. The men who worked on the new railroad crossing the country found them strong and warm. Farmers liked them, too. Levi ordered the canvas, which was off-white, from his brothers in New York. The orders grew larger and larger, and one time they ran out of the usual canvas. They sent another material, of equal weight but blue, that was from the city of Nîmes, France. The fabric came to be called denim (meaning *de Nîmes*—from Nîmes).

In 1873, Levi received a letter from Jacob Davis, a tailor in Reno, telling him of a change he'd made to Levi's pants. A customer had complained that the pockets weren't strong enough, and the seams kept splitting. He solved the problem by putting copper rivets in the seams, and he used orange thread in the pants to match the rivets. Levi and Jacob went into business together and called the new style of pants 501's. To this day the 501 remains the most popular style.

Levi Strauss became a wealthy man.

Since he never had a family of his own, he invited his nephews into the business. Together they expanded into making other products, such as overalls. Despite being a hardworking man who took pride in building a great business, Levi didn't believe that the point of life was to make money. He said, "I don't think money brings friends to its owner. In fact, the result is quite the contrary."

His impoverished childhood had made him sensitive to the suffering of others, and he worked hard at improving their lives. He created scholarships and prizes for children who studied Judaism. He also built homes for old people and orphanages for children. Levi Strauss is still a company that reflects its founder's humane and philanthropic values, which came from Judaism. The Torah, the Jewish Bible, teaches that giving to those in need is part of the Jews' contract with God. The Hebrew word for charitable giving is *tzedakah*, which means righteousness. It is a *mitzvah*, a commandment, to make the world fairer.

Levi died peacefully at home at the age of seventy-three in 1902, leaving his fortune to relatives, friends, and charity.

EMMA LAZARUS

JULY 22, 1849
TO
NOVEMBER 19, 1887

*I*n 1883, Emma Lazarus was one of several distinguished authors asked to write something special as part of a fund-raising effort for the construction of a pedestal upon which to put the Statue of Liberty. The womanly figure raising a lamp symbolizing freedom would be for millions of immigrants their first sign of America.

Despite the honor of the invitation, Emma declined it, saying that she didn't "write to order." First published when she was only seventeen, she was already a respected poet, playwright, and essayist. Along with other American writers in the mid-nineteenth century, including her mentor and friend, Ralph Waldo Emerson, she was creating a unique literary voice reflective of the country.

Like that of many women of her time, Emma's education came from tutors at home. She was an eager student, especially of literature, and quickly learned German, French, and Italian. Her prominent, wealthy family had been among the first settlers to arrive in America in 1654, and they moved easily in all social circles. Being a Jew meant belonging to a fine synagogue with other thoroughly American Jewish families.

Emma rarely wrote about anything Jewish at the beginning of her career. Mostly her work was about nature and heroic behavior from an American perspective. But in her mid-twenties, she felt that her work was trivial and too removed from the real world. She confessed to her publisher, "I have accomplished nothing to stir, nothing to awaken, to teach or to suggest, nothing that the world could not equally well do without." She was searching for meaning in her work and her life.

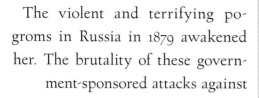

The violent and terrifying pogroms in Russia in 1879 awakened her. The brutality of these government-sponsored attacks against Jews, and the oppression of human beings by other human beings, shook the foundation of her sheltered life. Along with a committee of women, she went to Ward's Island in the East River, where Jewish immigrants fleeing pogroms were staying until they could find housing and work.

She saw thousands crowded together—men in long black coats praying, old women clutching shawls around their shoulders, mothers nursing babies, and crying, frightened children.

Moved by their suffering and their hope, Emma wrote a generous check and went to her friends for contributions to help these victims. Although the immigrants spoke a different language and were nothing like her, she felt kinship and claimed them as her people. While she helped many immigrants make a new life for themselves, they helped her, too. Through them she found her Judaism and her greatest creative inspiration.

She began to study Hebrew, and as she learned more about Judaism, she came to appreciate its rituals, especially the ob-

servance of the Sabbath, the day of rest. It promised a respite even for the poorest worker, making the weekly holiday a celebration of justice. She wrote: "The first star of the Sabbath eve restored to them their human dignity."

American democracy, Emma believed, offered Jews the freedom and tolerance necessary to live their faith. At the same time, she saw the need for a Jewish homeland—not so much for Jews like her who enjoyed social acceptance, but for the newly arrived immigrants. An early Zionist, she believed that without their own country, Jews would always be in the minority and would suffer the effects of prejudice.

America was wary of the hundreds of thousands of Jews arriving at its shores. Magazines and newspapers called it "the great Jewish invasion." Emma countered this response by writing poems such as "The Banner of the Jew" that called upon Jews to remember the power of their past and use it to guide their lives today.

Emma's work with immigrants changed her mind about contributing a poem for the Statue of Liberty. Their desperation and dreams inspired her to express what they longed to hear. Emma wrote a sonnet that she imagined the "Mother of Exiles" might say to the immigrant. These verses continue to speak for the highest hope and ideal of America:

> *"Give me your tired, your poor,*
> *Your huddled masses yearning to breathe free,*
> *The wretched refuse of your teeming shore.*
> *Send these, the homeless, tempest-tost to me,*
> *I lift my lamp beside the golden door!"*

The entire sonnet is written on the pedestal of the Statue of Liberty.

Early in her career, Emma worried that her work was unimportant and that the world could "equally well do without" it. She was wrong. By the time she died, at thirty-eight, she left words that have welcomed millions to America.

LOUIS DEMBITZ BRANDEIS

When Louis Brandeis was a teenager, he began collecting sayings. His favorite came from Ralph Waldo Emerson: "Every man takes care that his

NOVEMBER 13, 1856
TO
OCTOBER 5, 1941

neighbor shall not cheat him. But a day comes when he begins to care that he does not cheat his neighbor. Then all goes well. He has changed his market-cart into a chariot of the sun." Louis grew up not only as a man who didn't cheat his neighbor, but also as a defender of all who were being cheated.

He was born and raised in Louisville, Kentucky, and his earliest memories were of the Civil War. His parents, who had known injustice and oppression as Jews in Czechoslovakia, were openly anti-slavery in a Confederate state. "I remember helping my mother carry out food and coffee to the men from the North," Louis said. From his parents he learned the preciousness of freedom and the importance of taking the risk of standing up for one's beliefs.

The youngest of four children, Louis enjoyed the privilege of being born into a family that could afford to give him an excellent education. He entered Harvard Law School in 1875, following in the footsteps of his uncle Lewis Dembitz, a lawyer who believed that law was an instrument for rendering social justice.

Brandeis began his practice with former classmates who came from the most powerful families in America, and most of his clients became executives of big corporations. By the time he was forty, he was wealthy enough to defend only those whom he thought were right. "I have only one life," he said, "and it is short enough. Why waste it on things I don't want most? I don't want money or property—I want to be free."

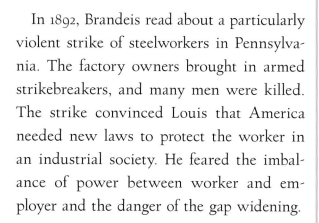

In 1892, Brandeis read about a particularly violent strike of steelworkers in Pennsylvania. The factory owners brought in armed strikebreakers, and many men were killed. The strike convinced Louis that America needed new laws to protect the worker in an industrial society. He feared the imbalance of power between worker and employer and the danger of the gap widening.

In 1910, his work took him to the Lower East Side of New York, where for the first time he met a very different kind of Jew. Unlike his family, these Jews were recent immigrants who spoke Yiddish and didn't read or write in English. They were garment workers protesting miserable working conditions, including pay so low that they couldn't feed their families. Even at the risk

of losing their jobs, they refused to work until their employers treated them fairly. By the time Louis met them, they had been on strike for three months.

Moved by the workers' courage, intelligence, and idealism, he helped them to negotiate wages and hours with their employers. For the first time in his life, he felt pride in being a Jew. "I have been to a great extent separated from the Jews," he said. "I am very ignorant in things Jewish. But recent experiences, public and professional, have taught me this: I find Jews possessed of those very qualities which we of the twentieth century seek to develop in our struggle for justice and democracy."

Turning his inquisitive mind to Jewish history and the Jewish future, he became a Zionist. "Every American Jew who aids in advancing the Jewish settlement in Palestine, though he feels that neither he nor his descendants will ever live there," he said, "will likewise be a better man and a better American for doing so." Impressed with the work of social activist and Zionist Henrietta Szold, he provided her with an income so that she could put all her efforts into building a modern Jewish state.

He also believed in a Jewish state because even in America, there was anti-Semitism. President Woodrow Wilson, wanting to reward Brandeis for his support in the presidential election, was unable to offer him a Cabinet post in his administration because of Brandeis's religion. However, Wilson ultimately succeeded in giving him a position that allowed him to leave a legacy of social justice when he made him a Supreme Court justice in 1916.

Known as "the people's lawyer," Brandeis was the first Jew on the Supreme Court. Establishing minimum wage, child labor laws, Social Security, and unemployment insurance are just a few of the ways Louis D. Brandeis made America a nation committed to protecting all its citizens.

HENRIETTA SZOLD

As Henrietta stood next to her father, Rabbi Benjamin Szold, waiting for the ship filled with poor immigrants from Russia and Poland to dock in Baltimore, Maryland, she thought of the sad, frightening stories her parents had told her about how much these people had suffered as Jews. One by one, father and daughter welcomed the people, and later they helped them find homes and jobs. Henrietta had trouble imagining what their experience had been, because America was a good place for everyone, including Jews.

DECEMBER 21, 1860
TO
FEBRUARY 13, 1945

The eldest of seven girls, Henrietta learned literature, science, and math in school. Her father taught her French, German, and Hebrew, and the great ideals of justice and equality. From her mother she learned that it wasn't enough to talk about what was terrible. You had to do something about it.

When she graduated from high school at sixteen, Henrietta longed to go to college, but her parents refused to send her. If she had been a boy, the answer would have been different. Instead Henrietta became a teacher in the high school where she had been a student the year before. She enjoyed the work, but she wanted to do more than teach privileged girls.

Henrietta turned her energies toward the immigrants who were arriving by the thousands each week. Many were alone and all of them were lost in America, not knowing the language or its customs. Henrietta remembered her mother's words and found a solution. She organized night classes for the immigrants to attend after work. She taught them English and gave them advice about how to get along in the new country. The first evening, thirty adults enrolled in her class, the next night twice as many came, and soon night schools began to spread. They became the way millions of immigrants from many countries learned English and became American citizens.

Although Henrietta felt safe and at home in America, she remained troubled about the growing anti-Semitism in Europe. One night in 1891, she went to a lecture given by a young Austrian named Theodor Herzl, who spoke of a solution. He said that the Jewish people could have a nation of their own in the land of the Bible—Palestine, as Israel was then called. Immediately Henrietta joined the movement, called Zionism, that worked to turn this dream into a reality.

In 1903, Henrietta moved to New York with her family, where she joined a small Zionist study group of women that met regularly to learn about the pioneers who were resettling the ancient land, read poetry, and send a little money to help the pioneers. Created around the time of Purim, the celebration of Queen Esther, whose Hebrew name was Hadassah, the group called itself Hadassah.

After her father's death and an unhappy love affair, Henrietta decided to heal her broken spirit by taking a trip to Palestine in 1909. She had expected that the journey would cheer her, but when she and her mother arrived, they didn't find the romantic picture of healthy, robust Jews building a new country but a place of great poverty and sickness. Most disturbing were the many young children suffering from an eye infection called trachoma, which led to blindness. It could be corrected with drugs, but nowhere in Palestine were the children being treated.

After they returned to America, her mother's suggestion that Henrietta's Zionist group send medical help to Palestine gave her a new purpose that would change her life and the life of the Jewish people. At first Henrietta was discouraged. Men dominated Zionist groups, and although they weren't accomplishing much, they didn't want women's influence. But she spoke passionately about Palestine, and soon she was recruiting new members and creating many Hadassah groups.

She described the trees being planted, the hunger for knowledge, and the new experiment in living called the kibbutz, where women had equal rights with men and the children were being raised together by the community.

In 1912, Hadassah became the first women's Zionist organization and chose Henrietta as its first president. Its motto, "the healing of the daughter of my people," from the Bible, became real when Hadassah raised enough money to send two nurses to

Palestine to serve both the Jewish and Arab populations.

When Henrietta was in her seventies, she once again saved Jewish children. Under her direction a group called Youth Aliyah rescued 22,000 children from Nazi-dominated Europe, where their lives were at risk, and brought them to Palestine to live on kibbutzim.

Despite the Arabs already living in Palestine who mistrusted the Jews' buying land and settling there, Henrietta believed that Palestine could be a new nation of peace created by both Arabs and Jews. She rented an apartment in Jerusalem, never buying furniture because she always thought that she would return to America. But Hadassah and the needs of Palestine kept her there until her death at eighty-four.

Although Henrietta didn't live to see the birth of Israel, her work lives on in Hadassah, the largest women's organization in America. Its world-class hospital in Jerusalem serves both Jews and Arabs, and it continues to be one of Israel's most important friends.

RACHEL "RAY" FRANK

APRIL 10, 1861
TO
OCTOBER 10, 1948

In 1890, on the eve of Rosh Hashanah in Spokane Falls, Washington, Rachel Frank did what no other Jewish woman in America had done before. She gave a sermon, and it was so bold, intelligent, and timely that a newspaper wrote: "Her words were dropping like sparks into the souls of aroused people before her." Ray Frank didn't set out to be a pioneer described as a "girl rabbi" and "female messiah," but her brief career as a persuasive and passionate female spiritual leader was an important step toward the first ordination of women rabbis in 1972.

Ray was a young journalist living in Oakland, California, when she went to Washington State to write a story about the new towns being settled there. When she discovered that there would be no High Holiday services because the Orthodox and Reform Jews in the area refused to worship together, she was shocked. A member of the Orthodox community who was familiar with her from her writings offered to organize services if she would give a sermon. She eagerly accepted his invitation.

Ray was well qualified to speak. She was born in San Francisco and raised in a home that loved and practiced Judaism at a time when women couldn't vote, let alone become spiritual leaders. After college, she taught in a public school and found that she had a gift for teaching and speaking publicly. She began to teach religious school and was so popular that adults sat in on her classes, too.

At the same time, she began writing for San Francisco and Oakland newspapers. Her letters to the editors of Jewish magazines attracted national attention. When she became the principal of the Sabbath

school of the First Hebrew Congregation, she began to see the problems of the Jewish community, particularly in its leaders. Criticizing Jewish leadership for its emptiness and materialism, she suggested that many Jews had forgotten that Judaism stood for principles and spirituality. She spoke out against the hostility between Jewish denominations and suggested that if women could be rabbis, they would bridge the differences.

The invitation in Spokane gave her the opportunity to demonstrate what a woman spiritual leader could do. When the local newspaper announced that she would appear at the Opera House, one thousand people, Christians as well as Jews, attended. A reporter described the event as the opportunity to hear "the one Jewish woman in the world, maybe the first since the time of the Prophets, to preach from a synagogue."

The High Holidays are a time when most Jews attend services and when the rabbi delivers a key message. Inspired by the gathering on Rosh Hashanah eve, Ray spoke powerfully what was in her heart and on her mind: for their own and their children's sake, the Jewish communities must overcome their differences.

She spoke again on Rosh Hashanah day and on Kol Nidre, the eve of Yom Kippur. She said: "My position this evening is a novel one. . . . To be at any time asked to give counsel to my people would be a mark of esteem; but on this night of nights, on Yom Kippur eve, to be requested to talk to you, to advise you, to think that perhaps I am tonight the one Jewish woman in the world, mayhap the first since the time of the prophets to be called on to speak to such an audience as I now see before me, is indeed a great honor . . ."

Her sermons demanded that Jews stop arguing about whether they wore hats or not, or whether they stood or sat down for certain prayers: they were all there to pray to the God of their ancestors. A Christian man was so impressed with her words that he offered land for a synagogue. Ray's sermons helped create the first permanent Jewish congregation in Spokane.

Ray was invited to speak all over the United States. As a woman, she was an outsider, and she took advantage of her freedom to say what she believed. She spoke eloquently and bluntly against the competition and divisions among Jewish communities, and she asked rabbis to help create peace.

She offered hints for success: "Give us congregational singing which comes direct from the heart and ascends as a tribute to God. . . . Give us simplicity in our rabbi, sympathy with things which practically concern us, give us earnestness, and our synagogues will no longer mourn in their loneliness."

Several communities asked her to lead them, but she declined, saying that she wanted to be "unfettered by boards of trustees and salary stipulations." After a decade of fame as a spellbinding preacher, Ray married and ended her career as a lecturer and public figure. Like a prophet, her words were a gift, as though she had no choice but to speak them. Her passionate words for Jews to "join hands in one glorious cause" still ring true.

LILLIAN WALD

MARCH 10, 1867
TO
SEPTEMBER 1, 1940

On a drizzling, cold March day in 1893, medical student Lillian Wald quickly followed a little girl through the muddy, littered streets of New York's Lower East Side. Already a nurse, Lillian taught a home nursing class to the mostly Jewish immigrant women who lived there, but she had never visited their homes. Shuddering from the stench of outdoor toilets and decaying garbage, she walked carefully up the slimy steps leading to a windowless two-room apartment where a family of seven lived.

The child's mother had been one of Lillian's students. She was bleeding uncontrollably and had sent her daughter for help. The woman was lying on dirty sheets soaked in blood, while the rest of the family, including children, were working at sewing clothes, pressing pants, or making cigars. Lillian bathed the woman, changed the bed, and showed the older children how to care for their mother. Their father was crippled and couldn't help.

What Lillian had seen shocked her. Relating her experience to her good friend and roommate, fellow nurse Mary Brewster, she declared that she would not return to medical school. There was a much more important task to do than work in a hospital: she wanted to live in the tenement neighborhood to bring nursing to an ignored population and to teach mothers how to keep their families healthy.

She persuaded Mary to join her in this heroic adventure, where they would not only heal the sick but also restore human dignity. They would help immigrants gain true citizenship instead of being "an alien group in a so-called democratic society." Lillian admired the immigrants for their courage, hope, and passionate desire to make a better life for their children.

Moving into one of few apartments with a private bath, the nurses announced that they would be on call day and night. Sometimes they gave medicine and sometimes they simply listened to people who no longer had parents, priests, or rabbis to guide them.

Visiting nurses existed at this time, but only for those who could pay or were of a certain religion, so few immigrants received health care. Lillian asked for ten cents from everyone so that patients didn't feel that they were receiving charity. With contributions from Jewish philanthropists, she hired more nurses and created a safety net for the poorest that would one day become a model for governments.

Lillian Wald's family had come to America long before the millions of persecuted Eastern European Jews who would arrive around the turn of the twentieth century. These were the people whose lives she changed, yet there was little in her background that prepared her for such work.

The Wald family had left Europe not because they were at physical risk from anti-Semitism but because they wanted economic opportunity and personal freedom. Settling in Rochester, New York, the German Jewish family prospered, and Lillian, along with her brother and two sisters, grew up comfortably with books, music, and a superb education.

At twenty-one, Lillian had enjoyed the life of a young woman accustomed to stylish clothes, elegant parties, and the many young men attracted to her warm, radiant smile. But she was bored. When her sister Julia suddenly became ill, Lillian watched the nurse who cared for her and decided that this was the work she wanted to do. Despite her parents' objections, she became a nurse in 1891.

In 1895, she created the Henry Street Set-tlement, a community center that brought health, educational, and recreational services to the Lower East Side, including celebrations of all religions. The nursing project she began with Mary led to the creation of public health nurses who provided affordable health care, and to the profession of social workers who taught the poor how to improve their lives.

While Lillian supported the rights of workers, women, and all who were oppressed, her particular concern was for children. She created the first classes for children with physical or mental disabilities, the first school nurses, and helped establish a Federal Children's Bureau that lobbied for an end to child labor.

Although Lillian had received a meager Jewish education and resisted religion because she believed it separated one group from another, she helped millions of Jews and lived Judaism's highest ideals of fairness and kindness to everyone. The Henry Street Settlement continues to serve its neighborhood, which is now Asian, African-American, and Latino.

HARRY HOUDINI (EHRICH WEISS)

MARCH 24, 1874
TO
OCTOBER 31, 1926

Ehrich Weiss was eight years old when his family left Hungary for Appleton, Wisconsin. His father, a rabbi, had little work in this part of America, where there were few Jews. Watching his mother cry when she didn't have enough food for her seven children made Ehrich wish that he could, like the magicians he loved to watch, snap his fingers and produce gold coins out of thin air.

Determined to make money, he ran away from home when he was twelve. After watching a magician pick up needles with his eyelashes, Ehrich practiced over and over until he could do it, too, and then he got his first job with a circus that was impressed with the trick. But he needed a bigger act if he wanted to make more than thirty-five cents a night.

Fascinated by the trapeze artists who seemed weightless as they flew through the air, Ehrich studied their every move and learned their skill. Wearing red stockings and a leotard, he became "Ehrich, The Prince of the Air," and soon joined the act.

At fifteen, he read a book by the nineteenth-century French magician Robert-Houdin that changed his life. Like Houdin, he wanted to become a legend, performing feats that had never been done before. He changed his name to Harry Houdini, and although he was still poor and unknown, every week he sent money home to his mother with a promise that one day she would be proud of him.

By the turn of the century, Houdini was attracting attention as an escape artist. He challenged the Chicago Police Department to lock him in a cell, handcuffed, boasting that he would free himself from

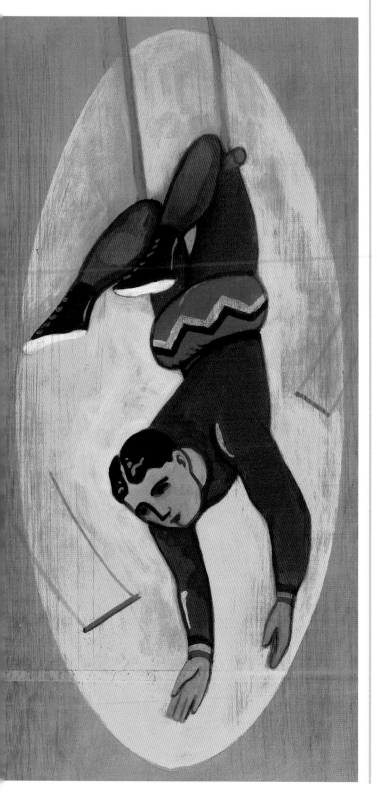

the jail. Taking off all his clothes to prove that he wasn't hiding a key, he even invited the police to seal his lips. Within ten minutes, Houdini strolled into the warden's office and handed him the handcuffs. His seemingly impossible escapes from coffins, safes, and jails, however, did not earn him the fame and fortune he desired.

An experienced showman gave him a tip. Houdini made his escapes look too easy; people thought that they were faked. He added suspense to his act by taking longer to escape. While the audience fidgeted curiously, he sat and read a book inside a trunk for several minutes before he appeared with his hair standing up, his face sweaty, and looking exhausted. People cheered loudly, and the crowds grew bigger.

Tens of thousands of immigrant Jews trapped by poverty and no education saw him as a hero, a Jewish superman who had escaped from the weakness and helplessness that Jews experienced everywhere, even in America. Here was a member of their family who knew secrets, fooled the world, and performed impossible feats.

Never content to do the same feats over and over, he continually challenged himself with increasingly dangerous escapes. In 1916, at the height of his fame, Houdini took his act into the street. He put on a leather straitjacket, a garment with over-long sleeves that tied tightly around him. As he hung upside down from the *Pittsburgh Post* building, five stories up, 20,000 people watched anxiously while he twisted and wiggled to untie the jacket. If he fell, he certainly would die. Three minutes later, he triumphantly threw his jacket to the crowd.

No one will ever know how Houdini, the greatest magician who ever lived, performed such unbelievable feats, but we know this: it wasn't magic but hard work. He turned his body into a precise machine that could go beyond what others could do. Even though he was only five feet six inches tall, he was amazingly strong. He ran ten miles a day, trained his toes to work almost as well as his fingers, and learned to hold his breath for four minutes. He never smoked or drank.

In the 1920s, "spiritualists" claimed to have supernatural powers that let them communicate with the dead. Houdini mistrusted them. No one knew better than he the difference between illusion and magic.

In 1926, on Halloween, he died at fifty-two, worn out from his work. He promised his wife that if there was a way to communicate from the dead, he would reach her. After waiting for years, she announced that Houdini was right—the dead do not communicate with the living.

Houdini, however, continues to live in every magician who came after him. He remains an inspiration through his amazing escapes and his belief that America offers the opportunity for anyone, even a poor Jewish immigrant, to succeed.

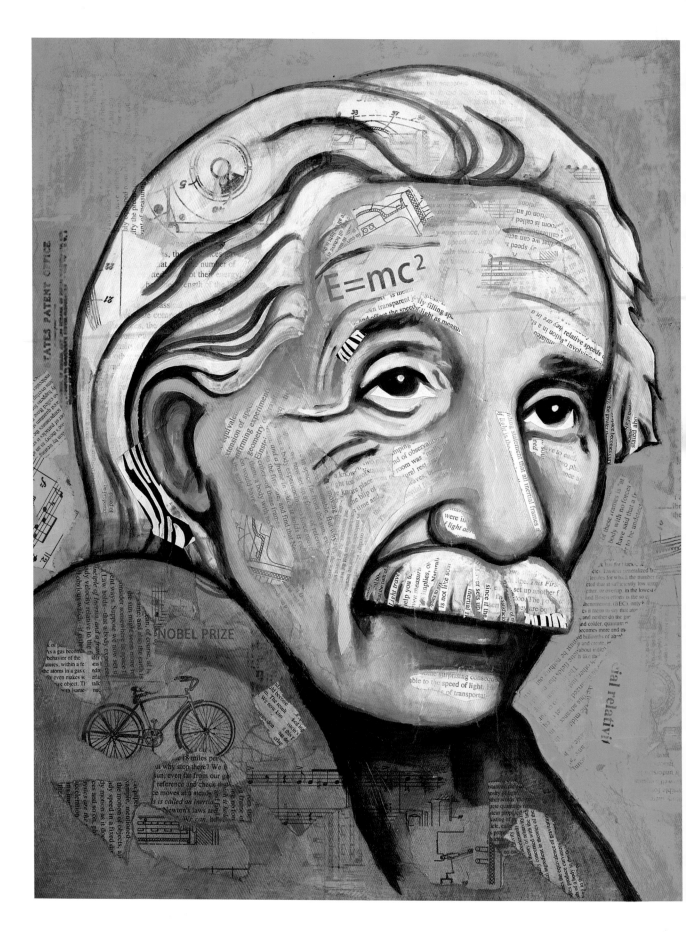

ALBERT EINSTEIN

MARCH 14, 1879
TO
APRIL 18, 1955

When Albert Einstein was five years old, his father gave him a compass. No matter how he turned it, the needle always pointed north. The idea that there were invisible forces in the world enchanted this child who had been slow to speak, who rarely smiled or talked, and who had a larger-than-normal head. His absorption in the compass relieved his parents. "He'll be a professor," his mother proclaimed.

Munich, Germany, in the nineteenth century, however, was not the right place and time for an unusual and sensitive child like Albert. Society valued conformity, discipline, and the worship of power. When a teacher posed a question to a student, he was expected to jump to his feet, stand straight as a soldier, and answer instantly. Because Albert took time to think before he answered, his teachers smacked his hands with a ruler. At fifteen, without discussing it with his parents, he renounced his German citizenship, preferring to be a citizen of the world than a member of such a rigid society.

Physics, the study of how things move and their relationship to one another, especially intrigued him. He continued his high school studies in Switzerland, a peaceful country where teachers were not feared but respected. After his college graduation, he became a Swiss citizen, working as an inspector of new electrical inventions and a teacher of physics.

In 1905, he presented a new idea in a paper that would later earn him the Nobel Prize, the highest award for a scientist. In it, he looked at light as energy made of billions of tiny particles called photons. This idea led to the invention of television, among other things. In

1916, he introduced an even more revolutionary theory, but it was so difficult that very few people understood it. The theory of relativity, best recognized by its formula, $E=mc^2$, envisioned the nature of movement in the universe in a completely new way.

Overnight, he became as famous as a movie star. Although no one knew what his idea really was, everyone in the world wanted to know about its eccentric creator, who didn't bother with wearing socks or getting his hair cut.

Fame gave Einstein the opportunity to speak his mind. He worried that schools

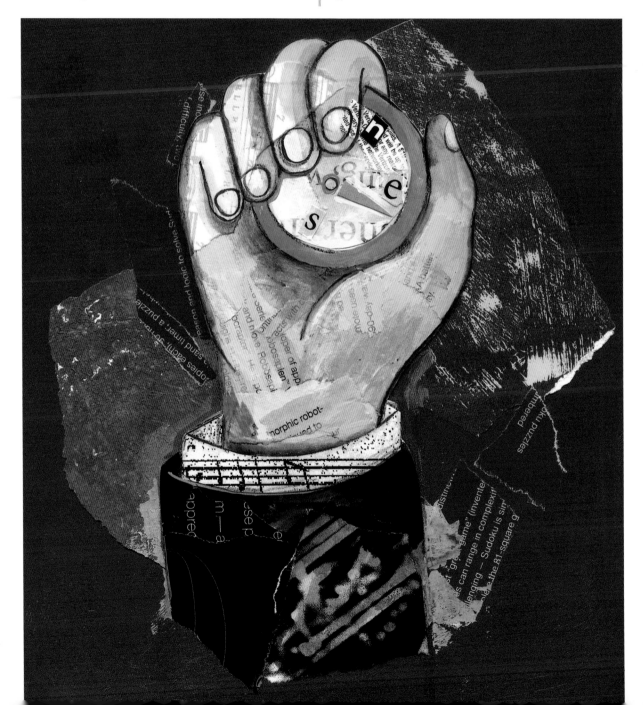

did more harm than good because they told children what and how to think. "Imagination is more important than knowledge," he said.

Even with his international reputation as the smartest person in the world, and *Time* magazine calling him "Person of the Century" for his scientific achievements, Einstein remained humble. He said, "I have no particular talent. I am just passionately inquisitive." His greatest worry was the misuse of science: "In the hands of our generation these hard-won achievements are like a razor wielded by a child of three."

Einstein was a scientist who believed in God, who loved the mystery of the universe, and who cared about people. "Many times a day I realize how much my own inner and outer life is built upon the labors of my fellow men, both living and dead, and how earnestly I must exert myself in order to give in return as much as I have received and am still receiving."

Despite his renown, Einstein, like any Jew in Nazi Germany, was in danger. In 1933, he left Germany with his wife, step-daughter, sister, and secretary and became a professor at Princeton University in New Jersey. Although he despised war and beliefs that separated people, he personally knew what Jews were suffering and helped the many who came to him. He wrote arti-

cles to raise money for refugees. He helped bring hundreds of Jews into the United States.

After visiting Palestine, he joined in the effort to create a Jewish homeland and was flattered by but declined an invitation to be its first president. Delighted to witness the birth of the state of Israel, he saw it as a chance for Jews to express their highest spiritual and ethical ideals.

During World War II, he heard from colleagues in Germany that the Nazis were experimenting with the creation of an atomic bomb based on his theory of relativity. After much contemplation, he wrote the president, Franklin Delano Roosevelt, warning him of the universal threat this meant.

America, concerned that thousands of its soldiers would die in the course of defeating Japan, had begun its own development of such a bomb. The United States dropped an atomic bomb on Hiroshima, Japan, on August 6, 1945, killing 140,000 innocent citizens.

Einstein was horrified that America was the first to drop the bomb: He had hoped that the Japanese would surrender when they discovered that the United States had the capability of using such a destructive weapon. Einstein spent the last ten years of his life speaking out against the horror of nuclear war.

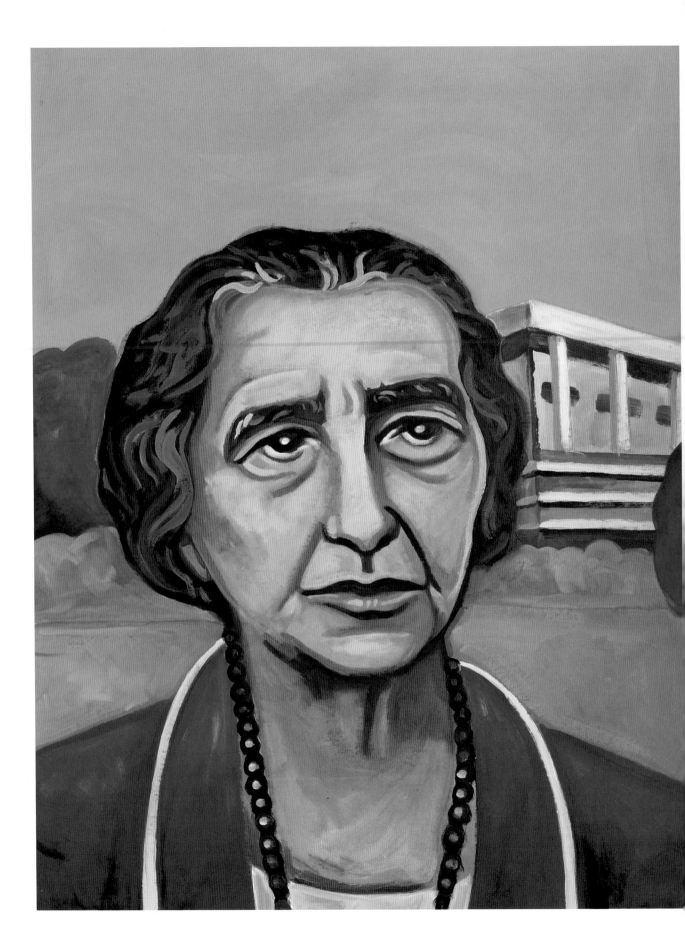

GOLDA MEIR

MAY 3, 1898
TO
DECEMBER 8, 1978

*L*ike a rock star, her first name was enough to identify her—Golda the social activist, Golda the Zionist pioneer, and Golda the prime minister of Israel. She looked like a grandmother and behaved like a lion.

Born in Kiev, Russia, Golda Mabovitch moved to Wisconsin when she was eight, taking with her terrifying memories of government-approved massacres, called pogroms, of the Jews. She also remembered the six graves of babies her family had left behind. In Russia, cold, damp, and crowded living quarters without enough food had taken her siblings' lives. Only Golda and Sheyna, nine years older, lived to see America.

Life in the new country was better but still difficult. Golda was always late for school because she had to help her mother in the family store. Sheyna worked in a factory until her weakened lungs required her to move to Denver, where the air was healthier. When Golda's parents wanted her to leave school at age fourteen to marry a man twice her age, she ran away to Denver to be near Sheyna.

Golda soaked in the fiery, beautiful words of Sheyna and her friends, and for the first time she was happy in America. They introduced Golda to the idea of a world without corrupt, powerful rulers who didn't care about workers, women, children, or Jews. They spoke about a Jewish homeland where Jews could be safe and could create a society of people working not only for themselves but also for others.

When Great Britain, the country that ruled Palestine, passed the Balfour Declaration in 1917, a promise to the Jews of a homeland, Golda was ready to live her new ideals. But it took four years before she and her husband, Morris Myerson, finally had saved enough money to sail for Palestine.

The Myersons moved into Kibbutz Merhavya, a small community where people worked side by side and shared everything they owned. Children were raised together with the help of many adults. While Golda happily planted trees, milked cows, cooked oatmeal, and bred chickens for the kibbutz, Morris wanted to raise their children traditionally in a small family.

The Myersons moved to Jerusalem, where Menachem and Sarah were born, but Golda wasn't happy. She loved her children, but she also wanted to be part of building the new country. She became a leader in the Labor Party and moved to Tel Aviv, the place of government. Although they didn't divorce, Golda and Morris never lived together again. Golda always regretted that she hadn't been a better mother to her children, but Jewish Palestine needed her, too.

By the 1930s, Jews were in danger. In Palestine, the Arabs wanted the settler Jews to leave and attacked them. In Germany, Jews were being tortured and killed. Golda went to France to meet with leaders from Europe. No country wanted the Jews. She said, "Let them come to Palestine. We're poor, but we'll gladly share the crumbs of our poverty with them." But Britain wouldn't permit it, fearing that the Arabs would turn against them. Before the war ended in 1945, millions of Jews perished. The Arabs continued to attack Jews in the Middle East.

In 1947, the United Nations divided Palestine into two states—one Arab state and one Jewish. While the Jews celebrated, the Palestinian Arabs went to war. For years, the British had sold guns to Arabs but wouldn't allow Jews to own them. Golda went to the United States to raise funds. "The spirit is there. But this spirit alone cannot face rifles and machine guns," she said. The Jewish community responded with a gift of $50 million.

On May 14, 1948, Golda wept as she signed Israel's declaration of independence. She was elected to the new legislature, the Knesset, and became Israel's first minister of labor. To mark her new citizenship as an Israeli and not a Palestinian, she changed her name to Meir: "to give light" in Hebrew.

Golda became prime minister when she was seventy-one years old. Despite her age, she was a vigorous leader who searched for peace as she prepared for war. In 1973, on Yom Kippur, Egypt attacked Israel, and thousands of soldiers died. Although Israel finally prevailed, many blamed Golda for not being better prepared.

She remains a hero, however, especially to women, and she never gave up her dream of Israel and its neighbors one day living in peace.

ABRAHAM JOSHUA HESCHEL

When Abraham Joshua Heschel was born, the Hasidim, the pious and mystical Jewish community of Poland, expected great things of him.
Descended from seven generations of charismatic rabbis, he grew up hearing magical stories about his ancestors. Many believers traveled long distances to learn from the legendary teachers and leaders who gave advice, decided disputes, and most of all, gave people the strength and faith to overcome their poor, difficult lives.

JANUARY 11, 1907
TO
DECEMBER 23, 1972

Abraham Joshua, named for his great-great-grandfather, was the youngest of six children. What Avremele, as he was called, enjoyed most was sitting on his father's lap, closing his eyes, and taking an imaginary trip to Mezbizh, the village where his father was born. His favorite adventure was to visit the house of the Ba'al Shem Tov, the first Hasidic master, who knew and taught the secrets of the universe.

The Ba'al Shem Tov could see the hidden sparks of God that glowed inside everything that was created. These holy sparks were the goodness God put into all people. When Abraham Joshua was a small boy, adults could see that he had the gift to find such goodness. He was treated like a prince. When he entered his father's synagogue, everyone jumped up to make room for him. By the time he was six, students of all ages listened to his teachings about Judaism and life.

Although his family was very learned about Jewish texts, they knew little of the world outside their small community. At fifteen, Abraham Joshua grew discontented with such narrow learning. He was curious about the wider world. Poetry and philosophy must have sparks in them, too, he thought. His mother, also from a family re-

nowned for its rabbis, allowed him to go to schools where he could learn math, science, art, and philosophy.

He eagerly entered the University of Berlin in 1927 to study art history and philosophy, and he loved his classes. He soon discovered, however, that the academic world was narrow in its own way. Every morning Abraham Joshua thanked God in his prayers for his mind, his eyesight, and for the miracle of his being alive. His professors couldn't see holy sparks anywhere and thought that God was at best an interesting idea.

The other challenge he encountered in Berlin was political. In the 1930s, Germany was becoming a nation that blamed Jews for all its problems. Jewish books were burned, synagogues were destroyed, and the government spoke openly of getting rid of all its Jews. Teachers who had once welcomed Abraham Joshua now shunned him. It took him three years to find a professor who would read his doctoral thesis about the Biblical prophets.

He wrote about the prophets as ordinary people without special powers of prediction. What made them different was their inability to keep quiet in the presence of injustice and cruelty. While most people accepted the world as it was, to the prophet indifference was evil.

While doing research in a library owned by German priests, Heschel asked the librarians why they weren't speaking out against the anti-Semitism of Nazi Germany. One librarian explained that if they protested, the Nazis would close their library and their precious books would be lost to the world. The priests valued books over human life.

Rabbi Heschel fled to America in 1940 and taught for five years at the Hebrew Union College, the Reform seminary in Cincinnati. During those lonely, frightened years, he learned that his mother and three sisters had been murdered in Poland. Meeting Sylvia Straus in 1945 helped him to keep his faith in holy sparks. They married and moved to New York, where Rabbi Heschel became a professor of mysticism at the Jewish Theological Seminary.

They had a daughter, Susannah, who remembers, "My father loved being a father." Although she isn't a rabbi, she follows in her family's tradition by being a professor of Jewish studies and a writer. From her father she learned that "God suffers when human beings are hurt, so that when I hurt another person, I injure God."

By the 1950s, Dr. Heschel had become one of America's best-known religious leaders through his books and lectures. His teachings helped people to experience God in their everyday lives, and he gave them a sense of a God who loves and cares about people as much as a parent cares about his or her children.

His experience in Nazi Germany made him outspoken about civil rights and the war in Vietnam. In 1965, he marched in Selma, Alabama, with Martin Luther King, Jr., a dear friend who reminded him of the heroes of his father's stories. Afterward he said, "I felt that my legs were praying."

HENRY BENJAMIN "HANK" GREENBERG

JANUARY 1, 1911
TO
SEPTEMBER 4, 1986

When Hank Greenberg, baseball's first Jewish superstar, was elected to the Baseball Hall of Fame in 1956, he said, "I've had many thrills in baseball. This, though, is the greatest." His thrills included being named Most Valuable Player (MVP) twice, being an All-Star four times, and being a four-time league leader in home runs and runs batted in (RBIs). In 1934, his batting average of .339 helped the Detroit Tigers go from fifth place to win the pennant for the first time in twenty-five years and begin their rise to becoming a championship team.

Many boys dream of playing for a major league baseball team, and for most it remains a dream. For a Jewish boy like Hank, whose immigrant parents thought baseball was for bums and wanted a respectable career for their son, it was almost unimaginable.

Living across the street from Crotona Park in the Bronx, New York, gave Hank a chance not only to learn baseball but also to fall in love with it. It didn't come easily, however. Hank, who would grow to be six feet four and over two hundred pounds, didn't look like someone who would become one of the greatest baseball players in history.

His high school coach described him as a ballplayer who "never played games, he worked at them. He wasn't a natural athlete. His body reactions were slow, and he had trouble coordinating his big body. He couldn't run a lick because of his flat feet. . . . I believe his size made him self-conscious."

His awkwardness wasn't limited to the baseball diamond. He hated the snickers he heard when he struggled to squeeze into the desks at school, and never had the answer to the question "How's the weather

[53]

up there?" Baseball became his refuge, and he put all his effort into it.

When an old-time baseball player who was watching him one day told him that he hit the ball better than Lou Gehrig, it was the first time Hank thought he could become a professional player. He was sixteen.

The most powerful team in baseball, the Yankees, played just a few miles from his home, but he rarely went to a game because his family couldn't afford it. He wanted to become a Yankee, but he knew that he wasn't going to replace their great first baseman, Lou Gehrig. So when the Tigers offered him $3,000 to sign a contract and $6,000 after his freshman year in college, he jumped at it. Even his father admitted that so much money meant baseball was more than a game—it was a business. Hank dropped out of New York University and took the first bus to Florida for spring training, but he didn't play well, and they sent him to the minor leagues.

At twenty-two, he was ready both emotionally and physically to play in the major leagues. When he reached Detroit in 1933, the Jewish community welcomed him like a hero, and he realized that he wasn't playing just for himself. He was a symbol of power and success for American Jews. One Jewish reporter wrote: "He was good, he was proud, and he was big!"

Although he no longer followed the Orthodox practice of his family, when the World Series in 1934 fell on Yom Kippur, he kept his promise to his father and didn't play. He walked to a Detroit synagogue for services, and the congregation stopped praying to applaud him.

The first baseball player to enlist in the Armed Forces in World War II, Hank went overseas and didn't return to his team until 1945, when he was thirty-four. He helped the Tigers win the pennant with a grand slam home run. In 1947, his last year in baseball, he met Jackie Robinson, the first African-American to play in the major leagues. Hank had special sympathy for Jackie Robinson because he had experienced prejudice, too. Hank told Jackie not to be bothered by bigots: "Stick in there. You're doing fine." Hank Greenberg was Jackie Robinson's hero.

Like Robinson, whose pioneering career made it easier for other African-Americans in baseball, Hank Greenberg led the way for future Jewish baseball players, such as pitching legend Sandy Koufax. Toward the end of his life, Hank said, "I want to be known not only as a great ballplayer, but even more, as a great Jewish ballplayer."

LEONARD BERNSTEIN

AUGUST 25, 1918
TO
OCTOBER 4, 1990

When Leonard Bernstein died in 1990, composer Ned Rorem wrote: "Was he too young to die? What is too young? Lenny led four lives in one, so he was not 72, but 288." The four lives referred to his multiple careers as conductor, composer, pianist, and teacher. Lenny, as he was best known, will always remain youthful in our memories, because he lived with exuberance, passion, and joy, especially when it came to music.

His mother said that when he was a baby, "I'd turn on a Victrola and play him a record and he would stop crying, like on a dime." As a little boy, when he went to the synagogue near his family's home in Boston, Massachusetts, the choral music and organ chords thrilled him. His father, however, wasn't happy about Lenny's love of music. He didn't want him to be a musician, because he thought it wasn't respectable and didn't pay well.

When Lenny was ten, his aunt gave the family an old piano she no longer needed. Lenny said, "I remember touching the piano the day it arrived, just stroking it. I knew, from that moment to this, that music was 'it.' There was no question in my mind that my life was to be about music." When he began piano lessons, everyone recognized his genius, even his father, who gave him a new baby grand piano for his bar mitzvah.

Lenny's parents, who had come from Russia with almost no education, were delighted when their son was accepted into Harvard University as a music major, especially since the school allowed only 10 percent of the student population to be Jewish. One of his professors,

Orchestra, he received a call early on a Sunday morning from the Philharmonic's musical director. Bruno Walter, the great German conductor, was ill. Could Lenny conduct the orchestra that afternoon at Carnegie Hall?

Although groggy from a late-night party, Lenny snapped awake, both thrilled and terrified. Assistant conductors normally waited years for such an opportunity, because conductors rarely missed a performance. The concert would be broadcast on CBS Radio to millions of listeners, and he didn't even have time to rehearse with the orchestra!

His whole family, including his eleven-year-old brother, Burton, was in the audience. As Lenny "advanced to the podium with the unfeigned eagerness and communicative emotion of his years," as *The New York Times* reported, everyone clapped politely. But the greatest applause occurred at the end, when, according to Burton, the audience "roared like one giant animal in a zoo." They jumped to their feet as Lenny came out to bow again and again. He was classical music's newest star.

Lenny led the orchestra without a baton, using his fingers as he played the piano, as well as his arms, head, shoulders, and even his knees. His face illustrated the emotion of the music. He said, "I share whatever I know and whatever I feel about the music.

composer Aaron Copland, urged Lenny to become a composer. At the same time, his teacher Dmitri Mitropoulos was sure that "genius boy," as he called Lenny, should become a conductor.

At twenty-five, Lenny became the first American-born conductor to lead a major symphony orchestra in the United States, with a debut as dramatic as his style. Three months after he was hired as an assistant conductor for the New York Philharmonic

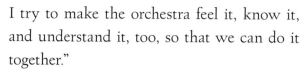

I try to make the orchestra feel it, know it, and understand it, too, so that we can do it together."

At the same time that Bernstein was a celebrity conductor, he was also composing both classical and contemporary music. He is perhaps best known for the music he created for *West Side Story,* the Broadway show about warring New York City gangs based on *Romeo and Juliet.* Lenny also wrote symphonies and created the popular Young People's Concerts for television, which introduced classical music to millions of children. These shows, filmed with an audience of mostly children, made music fun, with Bernstein's entertaining explanations of how sound inspires moods in the listener. For Lenny, music was an exciting adventure, and his enthusiasm opened the door to classical music for children as well as adults.

While Leonard Bernstein is remembered as the most influential musical force of the twentieth century, his world outside music included being a father, a Zionist, an author, and a civil rights activist. His personal life reflected his passion and creativity. A chain smoker, a lover of both women and men, he lived hard and fast.

Although Lenny wasn't as religious as his parents, he was proud of being Jewish. He went to Israel in 1948 to play for Israel's soldiers during the War of Independence. He conducted the Israel Philharmonic Orchestra in a desert, where the musicians balanced their chairs on the rocky terrain. Israeli prime minister David Ben-Gurion and 5,000 troops listened to Gustav Mahler's Symphony No. 2 ("Resurrection") and drew strength from the concert. In 1977, he conducted his composition *Kaddish* at the Leonard Bernstein Festival in Israel.

Some say that if he had concentrated his talents in just one arena, say composing, he would have been greater than Aaron Copland, or if he had only conducted, he would have exceeded Arturo Toscanini. Perhaps his legacy, however, was even greater. His music lives on in revivals of his shows, and because of his example, young conductors have become freer to express their emotions. His brother said at Lenny's funeral, "Descended from rabbis, he was a rabbi at heart, a master teacher." His best lesson was the way he lived his life, always doing what he loved most.

Equality of rights under the law shall not be denied or abridged by the United States or by a State on account of sex.

BELLA SAVITSKY ABZUG

JULY 24, 1920
TO
MARCH 31, 1998

"There are those who say I'm impatient, impetuous, uppity, rude, profane, brash, and overbearing. Whether I'm any of those things, or all of them, you can decide for yourself. But whatever I am—and this ought to be made very clear at the outset—I am a very serious woman." Bella Abzug wrote these words in 1970, during her first year in Congress. The first Jewish congresswoman and one of the most powerful activists in America, Bella told her daughters and other young women, "Never hesitate to tell the truth. And never, ever, give in or give up."

During her three terms, Congresswoman Abzug, one of nine women out of 435 members of Congress, introduced the first laws outlawing domestic violence and ensuring that parents could not take away their children's civil rights. Because of her example and her call to women, many more women became judges and took roles in government.

Speaking up came naturally to Bella. When she was eight, she asked her grandfather why, even though she knew all the prayers, she had to sit in the women's balcony in the synagogue. Her grandfather told her that was just the way things were. Unable to accept his answer, Bella kept asking until her mother said, "Enough!" But her mother would laugh and say, "She came out yelling," and Bella knew she was proud of her outspokenness.

When Bella was born, in 1920, in the Bronx, New York, women had just been given the right to vote. Her Orthodox, Russian-immigrant family had few luxuries, but they always had enough money to help others. From her parents, Bella learned that to be a Jew is to care about all people, especially the weakest.

When Bella was thirteen, her father died, and she was told that she couldn't recite the Mourner's Kaddish for him because she was a girl. For a moment she was sorry that she hadn't been born a boy, but then she recovered. Every day on her way to school, she went to the synagogue and recited the prayer for her father. "I just stood in the corner and prayed; the rabbi looked away," she said.

The rise of Hitler in the 1930s made Bella a Zionist and launched her career as a speaker and organizer. As a teenager, she found subway passengers ready listeners to her requests for a few pennies to plant trees and build houses for a Jewish homeland. More than a refuge, it would be a new society based on the principles of equality and justice for everyone.

Bella observed how unprotected her mother had been after her husband's death and how difficult it was for a woman to

support her family. Still, her mother set an example of independence that helped Bella make the decision to pursue a professional career. While Bella's other relatives told her to marry a lawyer, her mother told her to apply to Columbia University's law school. Bella graduated at twenty-four, the same year she married Martin Abzug.

Bella worried about whether she could be a lawyer and also have a family. In the 1940s and 1950s, most women had to give up their careers when they had children. Fortunately, she had married an unusual man for that time. Martin was proud of his wife's intention to work in defending the poor, and he shared the responsibility of parenting their two daughters.

Feminist Gloria Steinem once explained why her friend Bella had such extraordinary courage and confidence: "She had a mother who thought she should be president and a husband who thought she should be president."

When her children were nearly grown, Bella did what she had wanted to do for a long time: run for political office. The newspapers greeted her congressional campaign by calling her a "hell-raiser," nicknaming her "battling Bella," and comparing her voice to a foghorn. Many tried to disempower her, but Bella was popular with voters because she was warm, funny, and truthful. She also made politics exciting.

"We're going to start doing something for the millions of people in this country whose needs, because of the callousness of the men who've been running our government, have taken a low priority to the cost of killing people in Indochina," she told cheering crowds. "I'm going to work to stop it. I want to bring Congress back to the people." Reelected for three terms, Bella served from 1971 to 1977.

Until her death in 1998, she never stopped working for peace, civil rights, and, toward the end of her life, the environment. She set an example for women, Jews, and all human beings by demanding that we do a better job of caring for one another.

RUTH BADER GINSBURG

MARCH 15, 1933

Ruth Bader Ginsburg was sixty years old when she received a phone call that she will never forget. It was from President Bill Clinton, asking her if she would serve as a Supreme Court justice. This was the first time a Jewish woman had been offered the honor of one of the most important positions anyone could have in America.

Justice Ginsburg has a lifetime opportunity, as one of nine judges to sit on the Supreme Court, to interpret laws that make a difference in people's lives. She shares with her predecessor, Justice Louis Brandeis, a belief rooted in Judaism that law can and must make a more just and compassionate society. As Brandeis fought for the worker, so Ruth Ginsburg has defended women.

When the Senate met with Judge Ginsburg to learn more about her, she told its members how she had become sensitive to discrimination: "I grew up during World War II in a Jewish family. I have memories as a child, even before the war, of being in a car with my parents and passing a resort in Pennsylvania with a sign out front that read: 'No dogs or Jews allowed.' Signs of that kind existed in this country during my childhood. One couldn't help but be sensitive to discrimination living as a Jew in America at the time of World War II." Ninety-six senators out of one hundred voted in her favor.

When President Clinton introduced her at a press conference to announce her appointment, he described her as a judge who has always "stood for the individual, the person less well-off, the outsider in society, and has given those people greater hope by telling them they have a place in our legal system."

Ruth added her own words. She thanked her mother, describing her as "the bravest and strongest person I have known, who was taken from me much too soon. I pray that I may be all that she would have been had she lived in an age when women could aspire and achieve and daughters are cherished as much as sons."

Ruth was born in Brooklyn, New York, to a father who came from Russia when he was thirteen and an American-born mother whose parents were Polish immigrants. One of Ruth's early memories was going to the public library with her mother. Her parents had not been able to afford to go to college themselves, but they taught their daughter to love learning, to care about people, and to work hard for whatever she wanted or believed in.

During her freshman year at Cornell University, Ruth met her future husband, Martin. She had begun to think about law as a way to preserve the best values of America. She and Martin both decided to go to law school, figuring it would give them something in common to talk about.

Martin entered Harvard Law School a year ahead of her. Although she wanted to follow him, she hesitated. First, her characteristic humility made her question whether she was smart enough. Second, no one close to her, except her husband, thought it was a good idea. Why couldn't she be a teacher like other women? Besides, Harvard had yet to accept women into law school. Finally, she had a new baby to raise. In the end, she did apply and was accepted as one of nine women in a class of five hundred students.

When she graduated at the top of her class in 1959, she expected it would be easy to find a job. But her first encounter in New York was with Justice Felix Frankfurter, who flatly said, "I don't hire women." Major law firms wouldn't hire her, nor would law schools employ her as a professor. "To be a woman, a Jew, and a mother to boot, that combination was a bit much," Ruth said years later.

In 1963, she finally landed a position as a law professor at Rutgers University, becoming one of the first women to hold such a job, and began her career as an advocate of women's rights. By the early 1970s, she had argued six key discrimination cases that won rights for men as well as women. For example, she challenged the U.S. military's policy of giving larger maternity benefits to the wives of men in the service than it gave to husbands of women in the service.

President Clinton had met Ginsburg once only briefly. He invited her to meet with him shortly before he announced his decision to appoint her. A ninety-minute visit convinced him that her opinions and ideas would be valuable assets to the Supreme Court. She has continued to be an advocate for women's rights on the Court. In 1996, she wrote that the exclusion of women from a military institute violated their equal rights.

Known not only as a fair but also as a cautious jurist, Justice Ginsburg in 2000 was so strongly opposed to a Supreme Court decision that she stood alone in the force of her opinion. Because there had been so many uncounted votes in the presidential election in the state of Florida, the Court was asked to rule on whether there should be a vote recount in that state.

With a 5-4 opinion deciding that there could not be a recount, Ginsburg responded with "I dissent" rather than the customary "I respectfully dissent." This subtle omission expressed her extreme objection to a decision that threatened to mix politics—the majority of the justices were Republican—with impartial judgment.

Her dissent also reflected her vision of the ideal judge, about whom she said, "The greatest figures of the American judiciary have been independent thinking individuals with open but not empty minds—individuals willing to listen and to learn."

GLORIA STEINEM

Although her Jewish father didn't raise Gloria Steinem as a Jew, she says, "Wherever there is anti-Semitism, I identify as a Jew." For many years she has participated in a Passover of prominent women activists, which she credits as being the first spiritually centered occasion in her feminist life. Along with Ruth Bader Ginsburg, Betty Friedan, and Bella Abzug, she is part of a Jewish sisterhood that has fought for the world's largest oppressed population: women.

MARCH 25, 1934

Gloria's childhood was challenged by poverty, divorce, and her mother's mental illness. Because her father, Leo, bought and sold antiques across the country, for the first twelve years of her life Gloria never spent a full year in school. She and her family lived in a trailer. In her teens, she had the sole responsibility of looking after her mother, Ruth. Ruth's depressions and hallucinations ended her career as a journalist. When Ruth could no longer balance the claims of family and a job, Gloria had to become housekeeper, cook, and caregiver for her mother.

Suzanne, Gloria's older sister, convinced their father to look after Ruth so that Gloria could go to college. In 1952, the whole family, especially Ruth, delighted in Gloria's entering Smith College, where she majored in government and graduated with academic honors. After graduation, Gloria took a yearlong trip to India that changed her life.

India was the "place that opened the door to me," she said. It was a place with a rainbow of skin colors, in contrast with the United States of the 1950s, which kept white people "safe" from people of color. The poverty she witnessed starkly revealed the gap between the haves

and the have-nots. "America is an enormous frosted cupcake in the middle of millions of starving people," she wrote.

Upon her return, Gloria moved to New York to become a serious journalist. But in the early sixties, the only assignments available to women were articles for magazines like *Ladies' Home Journal,* about fashion, makeup, and celebrities. Because she had inherited her father's sense of adventure and her mother's love of the written word,

she found any kind of writing task easy, but she was frustrated. She wanted to write about things that mattered.

Her breakthrough came in 1963, when the editor of *Show* magazine asked her to be an undercover Bunny at the Playboy Club in New York. Gloria was not only smart, she was also beautiful, and this club, which catered primarily to men, quickly hired her to wait on their customers. For three weeks, she had to dress as a Bunny in three-inch spiked heels and a skintight skimpy costume with a white bunny tail, and she kept a diary that revealed how miserably the women were treated. Salaries were lower than promised, and they had to put up with men's insulting remarks and actions.

Steinem's story brought her overnight success, lawsuits from the club, and threatening phone calls. Although the magazine's editors appreciated the attention and increased magazine sales, they never gave her a serious assignment again.

Despite her fame, Gloria still couldn't get writing assignments about politics until a friend hired her as a political columnist for *New York* magazine. She wrote about civil rights, antiwar protests, and the peace movement. In 1969, she attended a public hearing on abortion, which was illegal at the time. She realized that the media wasn't covering it because women's issues weren't considered important. Her outrage moved her, through writing and speaking, to become one of the most important voices at the beginning of a feminist movement that included all women, not only white, middle-class housewives.

In 1972, Gloria co-created *Ms.* magazine, the first magazine for women that wasn't about food and fashion. How it happened was a miracle. As Steinem wrote: "Trying to start a magazine controlled editorially and financially by its female staff in a world

accustomed to the authority of men and investors should be the subject of a musical comedy." With Steinem's message and the help of her friends in publishing who announced it, *Ms.* sold out its first issue.

The magazine's intention was to awaken women to their full political, economic, and spiritual power. With a circulation of approximately 500,000 readers, it has helped women organize to create changes that are easily taken for granted, such as reproductive freedom and the presence of women in virtually every profession.

In the same year, along with Congresswomen Bella Abzug and Shirley Chisholm and feminist Betty Friedan, Gloria founded the National Women's Political Caucus to encourage women of all races to run for political office. The hope was that women would succeed in creating national health care and child care in America, the only industrial democracy without such a system.

Although best known as a feminist, Gloria has devoted her life to promoting racial, gender, and economic equality, fighting for reproductive freedom, building multicultural communities, and stopping violence, especially to women and children. Her passion and devotion to making the world fairer express the highest values of Jewish social justice and spirituality. The Jewish people are proud to claim her and are grateful that she claims them.

MICHAEL SCHWERNER
& ANDREW GOODMAN

When Andrew Goodman told his parents that he wanted to go to Mississippi in the summer of 1964 to help in a voter registration drive for African-Americans, they were proud but fearful. The world of Mississippi was very different from the multicultural and liberal New York community in which their son had grown up. Other civil rights workers had been met with violence in the segregated South. They were the enemy, seen as busybodies who deserved whatever happened to them.

NOVEMBER 6, 1939
TO
JUNE 21, 1964

NOVEMBER 23, 1943
TO
JUNE 21, 1964

At twenty-one, Andy wanted to act on the ideals with which he'd been raised, and to him no issue was more fundamental to justice for all than the right to vote. Although slavery had been over for nearly a hundred years, most Southern African-Americans still had to live in a world completely separate from whites, attending segregated schools and eating at segregated restaurants, and living in neighborhoods that often didn't have paved roads and streetlights. They sat in the backs of buses, had to use separate bathrooms and drinking fountains, and were sometimes beaten and even murdered without their perpetrators being punished.

At the beginning of the 1960s, young Northerners, many of whom were Jewish, became part of the civil rights movement to gain rights for African-Americans. By 1964, the movement was ready to take on Mississippi, the most racist of all the Southern states. Andy wanted to join the two thousand college students traveling to the South. He told his mother he was doing this "because this is the most important thing going on in the country. If someone says he cares about people, how can he not be concerned about this?" But she knew that the law would not protect him.

Goodman joined Michael Schwerner in Meridian, Mississippi, on June 20. Mickey, as he was called, was three years older and had been in Mississippi with his wife for six months working for an organization called the Congress of Racial Equality (CORE). He, too, was from a liberal New

York Jewish family, raised to believe that by sitting down and talking, everyone could come to see that all people are basically good and reasonable. He worked with James Chaney, a local African-American civil rights activist.

The notorious hate group the Ku Klux Klan had targeted Schwerner not only as a troublemaker but also as a Jew, and wanted him dead. On June 21, Goodman, Schwerner, and Chaney investigated one of the many black churches that had been burned to the ground after its members had been beaten. After seeing the damage and interviewing witnesses, they got into their car to return to Meridian.

The only way back was on a secluded highway. Going as fast as they could without exceeding the speed limit—the last thing they wanted was to be stopped by the local police—they approached a small town, Philadelphia, where the speed suddenly dropped from sixty-five to thirty-five. A policeman working with the Klan arrested them. Several long hours later, they were released late at night. They were nervous about driving in the dark but eager to get home. They didn't suspect that it was a trap.

Once again they were pulled over, this time by the deputy sheriff. Chaney, who was driving, was tempted to race past the sheriff, but Mickey thought it was better to stop. Later Schwerner's wife, Rita, explained why she thought they had stopped. "Mickey Schwerner was incapable of believing that a police officer in the United States would arrest him on a highway for the purpose of murdering him, then and there, in the dark."

The sheriff forced the men into his car, drove them to a deserted road, and turned them over to hundreds of his fellow Klan members. Mickey was dragged from the car first. "Are you that nigger lover?" a Klansman with a gun reportedly screamed.

With the muzzle of the gun pressed into his chest, Mickey answered softly, "Sir, I know just how you feel." A bullet went through his heart. The three bodies were found two months later in a pit. Seven men were convicted—not of murder, but of conspiring to deprive the civil rights workers of their civil rights. The men served prison terms of three to seven years.

Although Andrew Goodman and Michael Schwerner knew each other for only a short time, they and James Chaney died as brothers who believed in peace and nonviolence. All three lived and died with the belief that people are fundamentally good and the power of love can transform all human beings.

STEVEN SPIELBERG

DECEMBER 18, 1946

Steven Spielberg, one of the world's greatest filmmakers, was practically born with a camera in his hand. One of his earliest memories was playing with a home movie camera when he was four. A year later, his father took him to see Cecil B. DeMille's epic film about circus life, *The Greatest Show on Earth.* Steven had never seen a movie on a big screen before, and the images frightened him. "The people can't get out at you," his father reassured him.

But when a train wreck in the film showed lions and other animals escaping from their cages, the little boy felt as if the train had jumped off the screen and into his lap. Years later he said, "Ever since then I've wanted to involve the audience as much as I can, so they no longer think they're sitting in an audience."

Jaws, the film about sharks that made Steven a star in 1975, kept many people out of the ocean for a long time. It was a terrifying story of a great white shark that attacks swimmers in a seaside village. Few knew that the twenty-eight-year-old filmmaker, who had been making films for over twenty years, used three twenty-four-foot polyurethane sharks instead of a live shark because his actors were afraid of working with the real thing.

In the last thirty years, "Cecil B. DeSpielberg," as his mother called him when he was growing up, has made films about aliens, outer space, children, war, the Holocaust, and racism. Common to all his films are his fascination with techniques that create the illusion of reality and his drawing on vivid memories—good and bad—of his own childhood.

It wasn't only his love of movies and the machines that made them that led to Spielberg's career as a filmmaker. Making films helped him cope with loneliness. Slight and shy, he wasn't athletic, he didn't get good grades, and he often stood out as a Jew in the many places that his family lived while he was growing up. Whether he was in

Phoenix, Arizona, or Saratoga, California, making new friends was a struggle. His parents' divorce added to his isolation.

E.T. The Extra-Terrestrial, about a friendship between a lonely boy and a sweet nine-hundred-year-old creature from outer space that has been left behind on Earth, is his most personal film. Like Elliott, the boy in the movie, Steven felt different from everyone around him, and he invented imaginary friends. In E.T., Steven created a friend that both children and grown-ups wanted. When the film came out in 1982, it went on to become the highest-grossing movie up to that time.

After the birth of his son, Max, in 1985, Steven began to work on *Schindler's List*. "I don't think it ever occurred to me that I was actually going to make this movie until my child was born. Through the decision to try and expose my kids to Jewish history, I re-immersed myself in Judaism." His painful memories of being called names because he was a Jew left him fearing that Jewish persecution could happen again.

Up until *Schindler's List*, Spielberg's films had been primarily fantasies. He wanted to provide his audience with adventures. For this story, he said, "If I'm going to tell the truth for the first time, it should be about the Holocaust." He filmed *Schindler's List* in black-and-white, contributed most of the $23 million to make it, and never expected it to break even.

Considered by many not only his best film but also the finest dramatic film ever made about the Holocaust, *Schindler's List* tells the true story of businessman Oskar Schindler's efforts to save Jews in Nazi Germany. In 1994, after waiting almost twenty years for recognition, Steven Spielberg won an Oscar for Best Director. *Schindler's List* won seven Oscars in all, including Best Picture.

The film made Spielberg more committed as a Jew. From its profits he created the Shoah Foundation, dedicated to recording the stories of survivors for posterity. The foundation has also funded many organizations that promote tolerance. By practicing the principle of *tzedakah*, Spielberg is honoring the memory of the six million Jews who were murdered and turning memory into blessing by showing the destructiveness of intolerance.

Whether he makes films based on actual events or his wildest imaginings, Steven Spielberg entertains and inspires his audiences to look at the world in ways that will comfort them, inform them, and make them better people.

JUDITH ARLENE RESNIK

APRIL 5, 1949
TO
JANUARY 28, 1986

When Judith Resnik was born, travel to outer space was only a dream of science fiction. No one imagined an astronaut as a Jewish woman. Thirty-five years later, Judy Resnik made history by being the second woman and the first Jew to orbit the earth in a spaceship.

But being first wasn't what mattered to her. In one of her rare interviews, the intensely private astronaut said, "I've been the only woman in my profession for years. It's important for women to recognize that we cannot stand alone in the limelight . . . firsts are only the means to the end of full equality, not the end in itself."

To become an astronaut requires great intelligence, tremendous discipline, and a strong desire for excellence. As a young girl, Judy spent her time playing the piano, learning to read Hebrew, and solving difficult puzzles in math and science. Practice, patience, and self-control, along with her father's steadfast encouragement, enabled her to succeed at whatever she tried.

Whether it was reading all of the Nancy Drew books, baking cookies with her mother, or typing ninety words a minute, she devoted all of her energy to being the best she could be, but she never did anything to show off or get attention. It may be that she simply loved challenges, or perhaps working hard helped her to forget her parents' unhappy marriage, which eventually ended in divorce.

As a teenager, Judy never thought about being an astronaut or even a pilot. The only time she wondered about what was beyond Earth was in 1962, when the first NASA (National Aeronautics and Space Administration) satellite explored space. She asked her rabbi whether

Judaism encouraged such investigation of the heavens. He replied that human beings are made in the image of God and have responsibility for all of creation. Asking questions and studying in Judaism are even more important than having answers.

Of course Judy wasn't the first girl to be brilliant in math—she scored a perfect 800 on her math SAT test in high school—but 1978 was the first year that there was a special opportunity for her talent. It was the year she saw the announcement from NASA that for the first time, they were accepting women into the space program.

Like her grandparents, who had left Russia in the 1920s for a better life, Judy would be a pioneer. She called her father and said, "Daddy, I'm going to apply to NASA to become an astronaut." He told her, "Okay, you'll make it."

Judy trained hard to be chosen. She kept a strict diet and exercise schedule, and studied for a pilot's license. She cut her thick, curly hair to look more professional and met with former astronauts for tips about what NASA was looking for. She passed the rigorous physical and sailed through her interviews easily. Finally, after months of training and waiting, she was one of five women accepted into the space program.

In late 1983, after five years of training, Judy got the call she'd been waiting for: she was to be part of the crew on the first flight of the space shuttle *Discovery*. Just before the flight in August of the following year, she went with her father to the synagogue in her hometown of Akron, Ohio. The rabbi blessed her with these words: "May you go in peace. May you come in peace." People around the world saw the sign she carried with her into space that said HI DAD. Many remember her long dark, curly hair floating without gravity, like a halo, around her joy-filled face.

Two years later, she joined the *Challenger* expedition, a space launch that would receive even more media attention. One of the six other space travelers with Judy was Christa McAuliffe, a schoolteacher. It was the first time a nonscientist would voyage in space.

Of all the crew, Judy was the most helpful and friendly to Christa, even confiding that she got sick on roller coasters and that she had a fear of heights. Judy told Christa not to worry about the "vomit comet," a test ride for astronauts. "The men have the worst time with it," she said.

The *Challenger*'s launch was delayed for four days because of freezing weather in Florida. Finally it lifted off on January 28, 1986, at 10:37 A.M. As the shuttle left Earth, Judy Resnik exuberantly shouted, "All right!"

The greatest difficulty in being an astronaut for Judy was being a celebrity. Speak-

ing before groups of people was harder for her than flying at two thousand miles an hour in outer space. Judy once said, "I think something is only dangerous if you aren't prepared for it, or if you don't have control over it, or if you can't think of how to get yourself out of a problem."

The first minutes of a flight are the only time that astronauts aren't in control. Seventy-three seconds after liftoff, the shuttle began to zigzag, and then it disappeared. An explosion tore through the spaceship, killing all the crew members. Dr. Resnik was only thirty-six years old. There is a star, Judith Resnik3356, named for the young woman who is remembered for her courage, kindness, and humility.

DANIEL PEARL

OCTOBER 10, 1963
TO
FEBRUARY 2002

When Danny Pearl was ten years old, he liked girls, books, soccer, and writing. In his diary he confided, *I want to live a full life, and believe that I can. I want to be a book critic, but it doesn't sound very contributive to the world (I guess the only job that is is politics, which I wouldn't go into for anything).*

Despite his secure and happy life in Encino, California, he had fears. One day, while he was traveling in a car pool on his way to school, a terrifying thought came into his head. Even though he knew everyone in the car, including the driver, he was afraid that he was being kidnapped instead of being driven to school.

Twenty-eight years later, his fear came true. A journalist for *The Wall Street Journal*, he was living in India when the newspaper sent him to Karachi, Pakistan, to learn about Richard Reid, a man who had tried to board an American airplane with a bomb in his shoe. The United States government suspected that Reid had worked with violent Pakistani militants. Even though Danny and his wife, Marianne, were expecting their first child, as the South Asian bureau chief, he wanted to go and get the story. He made clear to his editor, however, that he would not take the dangerous risks he had once taken in the region, which was known for harboring many fundamentalist Islamic terrorists.

When Danny had graduated from Stanford University in 1985, he began his career as a hardworking, careful, yet brave journalist. He wanted to travel the world and learn about places very different from the privileged environment in which he'd grown up. The kinds of stories he enjoyed writing most were about people, not politics.

Wherever he went, he carried a mandolin—he preferred the violin, but a mandolin was less fragile—and a smile that told people he liked them. His passion for fairness, truth, and fun won him friendship and respect even from those who disagreed with him.

Although he had been in Pakistan for a year, it was only after September 11, 2001, that he discovered how many Pakistanis hated Americans and Jews. The attack on the World Trade Center had unleashed rage against the United States in poor Muslim countries. They saw America as favoring Israel over the Palestinians, their fellow Muslims. Since it was dangerous for Danny's full identity to be known, only a few Pakistani friends were aware that he was Jewish.

He and Marianne had planned to leave Karachi on January 24, 2002, the day after his appointment with the leader of the fundamentalist group to which Richard Reid was allegedly connected. With the baby coming, they preferred being in a safer place. Still, when they talked about whether they would ever settle down to a quiet life, Danny laughed and said, "No, we're going to change the world."

As he always did when he went out alone to an appointment, Danny arranged for Marianne to call him every ninety minutes to be sure everything was all right. When she called him at 8:00 P.M. on the night of January 23, his cell phone was off. After failing to reach him for an hour, Marianne began to worry. She agonized through a sleepless night, then called *The Wall Street Journal*, and the search for Danny began.

It ended four weeks later, on February 21, when his captors sent a shocking video of Danny's death, including his beheading. His enemies thought he was a spy for Israel, and they trapped him by making him think he was being taken to an important interview. They kidnapped this peace-loving man and killed him. On the video that millions saw, Danny, minutes before he died, no longer hid his identity. He said, "My father's Jewish, my mother's Jewish, and I'm Jewish."

Daniel Pearl died for no reason other than being an American and a Jew. It would have been easy for his family and friends to turn against Muslims, but they knew that if they did, they would be giving victory to hatred and fear.

Instead, they created the Daniel Pearl Foundation to help people of different cultures better understand one another. In addition to sponsoring an annual concert of international music, it has a Web site, www.danielpearl.org that shows that Muslims and Jews can work together. On it is a poem written by an Arab Muslim:

YOU WILL LIVE IN
EVERY HEART THAT
BEATS WITH LOVE
YOU WILL BECOME
A SWEET WORD
IN EVERY TONGUE THAT
SPEAKS THE TRUTH
YOU WILL BE A
SMILE IN MY FACE
AND YOU WILL BECOME
A LOUD CRY IN MY CHEST
A GREAT CRY
OF THE TRUTH
A CRY THAT WILL
NEVER CEASE.

Glossary

Anti-Semitism	Policies, views, or actions that harm or discriminate against the Jewish people.
Atomic Bomb	An explosive device whose destructive power is caused by the uncontrollable release of energy from the fission of neutrons.
Ba'al Shem Tov	Founder of the Hasidic movement in Poland. His name means "Master of the Good Name."
Balfour Declaration	A promise from the British government, written in 1917, that the Jews would have a homeland in the state of Palestine, which was under British rule.
Bar Mitzvah	A life-cycle ritual that occurs when a boy at thirteen is called to the Torah for the first time and becomes morally responsible for his behavior.
B'nai B'rith	The world's oldest and largest Jewish service organization.
Civil Rights Movement	A political movement begun in the late 1950s to assure that every citizen of the United States, especially African-Americans, has the ability to vote and live in an integrated society.
Confederacy	The eleven Southern states that fought in the Civil War.
Congregation	A group of people who have gathered together for a religious service.
Democracy	A form of government in which people are elected to represent everyone in a society.
Discrimination	Unfair treatment of one person or group, usually because of prejudice toward race, ethnic group, age group, religion, gender, or sexual orientation.
Domestic Violence	The use of physical force to injure a family member who is weaker than the aggressor.
Feminism	The movement dedicated to securing and defending rights and opportunities for women equal to those of men.
Fundamentalism	A religious movement that wants to return to its original principles, encourages strictness of practice, and understands things just as they are written—e.g., that the world was created in seven days.

HASIDIM	Pious and mystical Jews in Eastern Europe who lived from the eighteenth century to the middle of the twentieth. The Holocaust [see below] destroyed their community.
HIGH HOLIDAYS	Rosh Hashanah and Yom Kippur, the two most important holidays in the Jewish year; they come in the fall.
HOLOCAUST	The systematic extermination of six million European Jews, as well as Gypsies, homosexuals, and political enemies, by the Nazis in World War II.
INTEREST	Money charged to people who borrow money.
KIBBUTZ	A communal farm or factory in Israel run collectively in which people live and work together.
LIBERAL	Favoring political reforms that extend democracy, distribute wealth more evenly, and protect the personal freedom of the individual.
LOWER EAST SIDE	A neighborhood in Manhattan, New York, where many immigrants settled when they first arrived in America.
MINIMUM WAGE	The least amount of money an employer may legally pay a worker.
MOURNER'S KADDISH	Prayer recited for the dead. A child says it daily for a parent for eleven months after the death of a parent.
MYSTICISM	The belief that people can communicate with God through prayer rather than rational thought.
ORDINATION	A ceremony in which somebody is given the title, rights, and responsibilities of a rabbi or minister.
ORTHODOX	The most traditional movement in Judaism.
PALESTINE	One of the several names for the region between the Mediterranean Sea and the Jordan River and various adjoining lands.
PEDDLER	Someone who travels from place to place selling goods.
PHILANTHROPY	A desire to improve the material, social, and spiritual well-being of others by offering financial help.
POGROM	A government-sponsored physical attack on Jews in Eastern Europe.
RABBI	A spiritual leader in Judaism.
REFORM	A movement begun in the nineteenth century to make Judaism more modern and less governed by ancient law.
ROSH HASHANAH	The Jewish New Year.

SEGREGATION	The usually discriminatory practice of keeping ethnic, racial, or religious groups separate, especially by enforcing the use of separate schools, transportation, and housing.
SEPHARDIM	Jews originally from the Middle East and Africa who had been expelled from Spain in 1492.
SHABBAT	Also Sabbath. The weekly Jewish holiday that celebrates creation and is the day of rest.
SOCIAL JUSTICE	The principle of creating a society that makes an unfair world more just by protecting the weak.
SOCIAL SECURITY	A government program that pays out money to workers when they retire, provided they have reached a certain age.
SONNET	A fourteen-line poem with a special rhyme scheme.
SPIRITUAL LEADER	A person who leads religious services, teaches others the principles of kindness and justice, and tries to be a good person as a model for others.
STRIKE	The refusal to work by workers who want better conditions from employers.
SUPREME COURT	The highest court in the United States, which interprets the most important laws, and decides difficult legal questions.
SYNAGOGUE	Jewish house of worship.
TENEMENT	A large apartment building where, typically, many poor people live.
THEORY OF RELATIVITY	Einstein's theory that space and time are relative concepts rather than absolute concepts, an idea that envisioned a new way to understand the nature of movement in the universe.
UNEMPLOYMENT INSURANCE	Money provided to unemployed workers, especially those who have been laid off.
YIDDISH	The everyday language spoken by Eastern Europeans that is a mixture of German and Hebrew.
YOM KIPPUR	The Day of Atonement, the holiest day of the Jewish year, when Jews pray and ask for God's forgiveness.
ZIONIST	One who supports the Jewish homeland, Israel.

JEWISH-AMERICAN HISTORY TIMELINE

1730	New York Jews build North America's first synagogue, Shearith Israel.
1730s to 1750s	Jewish communities established in Savannah, Georgia; Charleston, South Carolina; Philadelphia, Pennsylvania; and Newport, Rhode Island.
1760	The first English prayerbook for High Holidays is published in New York.
1763	Jews in Newport, Rhode Island, dedicate the Touro Synagogue, the only surviving Colonial synagogue structure in America.
1776	Jews divide over the American Revolution, although most favor independence.
1787	Gershom Mendes Seixas, rabbi of New York's Jewish congregation, is invited to George Washington's inaugural.
1788	The ratification of the Constitution permits Jews to hold office.
1824	The Society of Reformed Israelites is established in Charleston, South Carolina.
1838	Rebecca Gratz establishes America's first Jewish Sunday school in Philadelphia.
1840	Abraham Rice, America's first ordained rabbi, emigrates from Bavaria to Baltimore, Maryland.
1849	High Holiday services are held in a tent in San Francisco, California.
1853	Isaac Leeser publishes his translation of the Bible into English. It is the first complete English translation.
1860	Rabbi Morris Raphall becomes the first Jewish clergyman to deliver a prayer at the opening session of Congress.
1862	Judah P. Benjamin is appointed Secretary of State of the Confederacy.
1866	The Ku Klux Klan is organized to maintain "white supremacy." The first rabbinical school in America, Maimonides College, is founded in Philadelphia.

1875	Isaac Mayer Wise founds Hebrew Union College, the rabbinical seminary of the Reform movement, in Cincinnati, Ohio.
1876	Emil Berliner's invention of the microphone makes the telephone practical and the radio possible.
1881	Pogroms and anti-Jewish legislation in Russia after the assassination of Alexander II cause thousands of Jews to leave the country.
1886	Samuel Gompers is elected the first president of the American Federation of Labor.
1886	The Jewish Theological Seminary is founded in New York City as the training ground for Conservative rabbis.
1888	The Jewish Publication Society is founded as part of a renaissance of American Jewish life.
1890	Ray Frank, the first Jewish-American woman to give a sermon, gets national attention for her High Holidays address.
1893	The National Council of Jewish Women is founded in Chicago.
1895	Lillian Wald creates the Henry Street Settlement.
1898	The Federation of American Zionists is established in New York.
1903	Emma Lazarus's poem "The New Colossus" (1883) is added to the pedestal of the Statue of Liberty in New York Harbor.
1906	Oscar Straus is appointed Secretary of Labor and Commerce, the first Jew to hold a Cabinet position.
1912	Henrietta Szold founds Hadassah, the women's Zionist organization. Anarchist Emma Goldman is deported.
1913	The trial of Leo Frank in Atlanta leads to the founding of the Anti-Defamation League of B'nai B'rith.
1916	Louis D. Brandeis becomes America's first Jewish Supreme Court justice.
1918	President Woodrow Wilson announces America's approval of the Balfour Declaration, issued by Great Britain in 1917 favoring the establishment of a Jewish homeland in Palestine.

1920	The 19th Amendment to the Constitution grants women the right to vote.
1921	Albert Einstein wins the Nobel Prize in Physics.
1922	Reconstructionist Rabbi Mordecai Kaplan's daughter Judith becomes a bat mitzvah, the first in history.
1925	Edna Ferber is the first American Jew to win the Pulitzer Prize in fiction.
1927	Warner Bros. produces a drama of Jewish assimilation, The Jazz Singer. The National Conference of Christians and Jews is established. It promotes an image of an America where all religions can be practiced.
1933	Albert Einstein leaves Nazi Germany to reside in the United States.
1938	The Fair Labor Standards Act enforces the five-day, forty-hour week in many industries. Instead of having to choose between the American pattern of work and the Jewish day of rest, increasing numbers of Jews can embrace both.
1939	David Sarnoff introduces television at the New York World's Fair.
1942	In New York, Rabbi Stephen S. Wise announces the mass murder of two million European Jews by the Nazis. A day of mourning is held on December 2.
1943	Hundreds of Orthodox rabbis march on Washington, seeking immediate rescue efforts to save the Jews of Europe.
1945	America drops atomic bombs on Hiroshima and Nagasaki, Japan, ending World War II.
1948	The State of Israel declares its independence and is recognized by President Harry S. Truman within its first hour of existence. Brandeis University is founded as the first nonsectarian, Jewish-sponsored institution of higher learning.
1954	Jonas Salk develops the polio vaccine.
1956	Hank Greenberg is elected to the Baseball Hall of Fame.
1958	The bombing of Atlanta's oldest and most prestigious Reform temple, in response to its rabbi's call for racial justice, caps a series of violent attacks by extreme segregationists against Jewish institutions in the South.
1964	Three civil rights workers—Andrew Goodman, Michael Schwerner, and James Chaney, are murdered in Mississippi.

1965	Abraham Joshua Heschel walks arm in arm with Martin Luther King, Jr. and other black leaders during the civil rights march from Selma to Montgomery, Alabama.
1969	Golda Meir becomes prime minister of Israel.
1970	Bella Abzug is elected to the House of Representatives.
1972	Hebrew Union College ordains Sally J. Priesand the first woman rabbi. Ms. magazine publishes its first issue.
1978	Yiddish writer Isaac Bashevis Singer receives the Nobel Prize.
1985	The first Conservative woman rabbi, Amy Eilberg, is ordained.
1986	The space shuttle Challenger explodes. Judith Resnik is killed with six other astronauts.
1993	The United States Holocaust Memorial Museum is opened in Washington, D.C. The film Schindler's List, directed by Steven Spielberg, is released. Ruth Bader Ginsburg becomes a Supreme Court justice.
2000	Senator Joseph Lieberman is nominated for the vice presidency on the Democratic party ticket, the first Jew ever to be nominated for this post by a major political party.
2002	Journalist Daniel Pearl is murdered in Karachi, Pakistan.
2004	Jews celebrate 350 years of American Jewish history.

BIBLIOGRAPHY

Brody, Seymour "Sy." *Jewish Heroes of America: 110 True Stories of American Jewish Heroism.* Delray Beach, Fla.: RSB Publishers, 1995.

Cagin, Seth, and Philip Dray. *We Are Not Afraid: The Story of Goodman, Schwerner, and Chaney and the Civil Rights Campaign for Mississippi.* New York: Bantam Books, 1988.

Encyclopaedia Judaica. Jerusalem: Keter Publishing House Jerusalem Ltd., 1972 and updates.

Feldberg, Michael, ed. *Blessings of Freedom: Chapters in American Jewish History.* Hoboken, N.J.: KTAV Publishing House / The American Jewish Historical Society, 2002.

Heilbrun, Carolyn G. *The Education of a Woman: The Life of Gloria Steinem.* New York: Ballantine Books, 1995.

Hertzberg, Arthur. *The Jews in America: Four Centuries of an Uneasy Encounter: A History.* New York: Simon & Schuster, 1989.

Huie, William Bradford. *Three Lives for Mississippi.* Jackson: University Press of Mississippi, 2000.

Hyman, Paula E., and Deborah Dash Moore, eds. *Jewish Women in America: An Historical Encylopedia.* New York and London: Routledge / The American Jewish Historical Society, 1998.

Lévy, Bernard-Henri. *Who Killed Daniel Pearl?.* Hoboken, N.J.: Melville House Publishing, 2003.

McBride, Joseph. *Steven Spielberg: A Biography.* New York: Da Capo Press, 1999.

Merriam, Eve. *Emma Lazarus Rediscovered: A Biography with Selections from Her Writings.* New York: Biblio Press, 1998.

Myers, Paul. *Leonard Bernstein.* London: Phaidon Press, 1998.

Nies, Judith. *Nine Women: Portraits from the American Radical Tradition.* Berkeley, Calif.: University of California Press, 1977, 2002.

Pearl, Marianne, and Sarah Crichton. *A Mighty Heart: The Brave Life and Death of My Husband, Danny Pearl.* New York: Scribner, 2003.

Sarna, Jonathan D. *American Judaism: A History.* New Haven, Conn.: Yale University Press, 2004.

Shapiro, Michael. *The Jewish 100: A Ranking of the Most Influential Jews of All Time.* New York: Carol Publishing Group, 1995.

Steinem, Gloria. *Outrageous Acts and Everyday Rebellions.* New York: Henry Holt and Company, 1995 second edition.

SUGGESTED READING

(FOR AGES 10 AND UP)

Adler, David A. *Our Golda: The Story of Golda Meir.* New York: Puffin Books, 1986.

Berkow, Ira. *Hank Greenberg: Hall-of-Fame Slugger.* Philadelphia: The Jewish Publication Society, 2001/5761.

Bernstein, Joanne E., and Rose Blue. *Judith Resnik: Challenger Astronaut.* New York: Dutton Children's Books, 1990.

Borland, Kathryn Kilby, and Helene Ross Speicher. *Harry Houdini: Young Magician.* New York: Aladdin Paperbacks, 1991.

Calaprice, Alice, ed. *Dear Professor Einstein: Albert Einstein's Letters to and from Children.* New York: Barnes & Noble Books, 2002.

Eiseman, Alberta. *Rebels and Reformers: Biographies of Four Jewish Americans: Uriah Phillips Levy, Ernestine L. Rose, Louis D. Brandeis, and Lillian D. Wald.* New York: Doubleday & Company, 1976.

Faber, Doris. *Bella Abzug.* New York: Lothrop, Lee & Shepard Company, 1976.

Ferber, Elizabeth. *Steven Spielberg: A Biography.* Philadelphia: Chelsea House Publishers, 1997.

Gross, David C. *A Justice for All the People: Louis D. Brandeis.* New York: Lodestar Books, 1987.

Henry, Sondra, and Emily Taitz. *One Woman's Power: A Biography of Gloria Steinem.* Minneapolis: Dillon Press, 1987.

Hurwitz, Johanna. *Leonard Bernstein: A Passion for Music.* Philadelphia and Jerusalem: The Jewish Publication Society, 1993.

Kevles, Bettyann Holtzmann. *Almost Heaven: The Story of Women in Space*. New York: Basic Books/ Perseus Books Group, 2003.

Krantz, Hazel. *Daughter of My People: Henrietta Szold and Hadassah*. New York: Lodestar Books, 1987.

Kraske, Robert. *Harry Houdini: Master of Magic*. Champaign, Ill.: Garrard Publishing Company, 1973; New York: Scholastic Paperbacks, 1989.

Kustanowitz, Shulamit E. *Henrietta Szold: Israel's Helping Hand*. New York: Viking Penguin, 1990.

Lazo, Caroline Evensen. *Gloria Steinem: Feminist Extraordinaire*. Minneapolis: Lerner Publications Company, 1998.

——*Leonard Bernstein: In Love with Music*. Minneapolis: Lerner Publications Company, 2003.

Levinson, Nancy Smiler. *I Lift My Lamp: Emma Lazarus and the Statue of Liberty*. New York: Dutton Children's Books, 1986.

Lynn, Erwin. *The Jewish Baseball Hall of Fame*. New York: Shapolsky Publishers, 1986.

McPherson, Stephanie Sammartino. *Ordinary Genius: The Story of Albert Einstein*. Minneapolis: Carolrhoda Books, 1995.

Merriam, Eve. *The Voice of Liberty: The Story of Emma Lazarus*. New York: Farrar, Straus & Cudahy/ The Jewish Publication Society, 1959.

Powers, Tom. *Steven Spielberg*. Minneapolis: Lerner Publications Company, 2000.

Rau, Dana Meachen. *Harry Houdini: Master Magician*. New York and London: Franklin Watts, 2001.

Roberts, Jack L. *Ruth Bader Ginsburg: Supreme Court Justice*. Brookfield, Conn.: The Millbrook Press, 1994.

Rose, Or N. *Abraham Joshua Heschel: Man of Spirit, Man of Action*. Philadelphia: The Jewish Publication Society, 2003.

Segal, Sheila. *Women of Valor: Stories of Great Jewish Women Who Helped Shape the Twentieth Century*. West Orange, N.J.: Behrman House, 1996.

Taitz, Emily, and Sondra Henry. *Remarkable Jewish Women: Rebels, Rabbis, and Other Women from Biblical Times to the Present*. Philadelphia and Jerusalem: The Jewish Publication Society, 1996.

Van Steenwyk, Elizabeth. *Levi Strauss: The Blue Jeans Man*. New York: Walker and Company, 1988.

Weidt, Maryann N. *Mr. Blue Jeans: A Story About Levi Strauss*. Minneapolis: Carolrhoda Books, 1990.

Wise, William. *Albert Einstein: Citizen of the World*. New York: Farrar, Straus & Cudahy/The Jewish Publication Society, 1960.